Jean Renvoize

Children in Danger

The Causes and Prevention of Baby Battering

Penguin Books

Penguin Books Ltd,
Harmondsworth, Middlesex, England
Penguin Books Inc.,
7110 Ambassador Road, Baltimore, Maryland 21207, U.S.A.
Penguin Books Australia Ltd,
Ringwood, Victoria, Australia
Penguin Books Canada Ltd,
41 Steelcase Road West, Markham, Ontario, Canada
Penguin Books (N.Z.) Ltd,
182–190 Wairau Road, Auckland 10, New Zealand

First published by Routledge & Kegan Paul 1974
Published with minor revisions in Penguin Books 1975
Copyright © Jean Renvoize, 1974, 1975

Made and printed in Great Britain by
Hazell Watson & Viney Ltd,
Aylesbury, Bucks
Set in Linotype Pilgrim

To Andrew and Alison

Contents

Acknowledgements

It would have been impossible for me to write this book without the generous help of many doctors, psychiatrists, social workers, police and local government officers. Out of extremely busy lives they nevertheless managed to find time to talk about their own specialized fields and to discuss the many problems arising in the management of baby battering cases. For professional reasons most have to remain anonymous, as do the parents who were able to overcome their natural reticence and tell me their own frequently painful stories. To all of these people I would like to express my gratitude and my debt.

In particular I would like to thank Ray Castle, Head of the NSPCC's National Advisory Centre on the Battered Child, who gave me endless help including reading the final manuscript and making several invaluable suggestions. I would also like to thank his staff, whose words I have quoted and whose experience I have drawn on. Also of great help has been Detective Superintendent Roy of the Northamptonshire Police and their principal police surgeon, Dr H. de la Haye Davies, who has given me constant assistance and encouragement. Dr A. Jackson, Consultant Paediatrician of the London Hospital, gave me much helpful advice and information, as did Ruth Johns of the Family First Trust. I would also like to thank Margaret Cruft who has given me much useful information.

Dr Henry Kempe of the University of Colorado Medical Center, whose work is frequently referred to throughout the book, has very kindly given me permission to quote from a broadcast he gave. I would also like to thank Dr Kempe and his colleagues, together with their publishers, for permission to reprint extracts from their two books, *The Battered Child*, published by the University of Chicago Press, and *Helping the*

Battered Child and his Family, published by J. B. Lippincott & Co. and by Basil Blackwell & Mott Ltd.

I would like to thank the authors and publishers concerned for permission to quote extracts from the following works: Joan Court, 'Psychosocial factors in child battering' in *Journal of the Medical Women's Federation*; Joan Court and Wendy Robinson, 'The battered child syndrome' in *Midwives Chronicle and Nursing Notes*; Carolyn Okell, 'The battered child – a tragic breakdown in parental care?' in *Midwife and Health Visitor*, 'Childhood accidents and child abuse' in *Community Medicine* and 'The battered child syndrome', in *Law Society's Gazette*; Dr J. M. Cameron, 'The battered baby syndrome' in *Practitioner*; Dr M. H. Hall, 'Non-accidental injuries in children', a paper read before the Health Congress of the Royal Society of Health; and Anthony Storr, *Human Aggression*, Penguin Books. I would also like to thank the Home Office for permission to reprint material from a memorandum, and *The Times*, *Guardian* and *Daily Mirror*, all of whom have given permission for extracts from articles.

Finally I would like to thank my family: my husband for encouraging me to write this book in the first place and for his continued support, and above all my two children, Andrew and Alison, for putting up with me while I struggled to learn how to be a mother, and who in spite of my shortcomings have come out of the experience looking remarkably cheerful.

Introduction

When I first began work on this book two years ago baby battering was a subject that had gained little attention in Britain. From time to time a child's death or maiming would be reported in the newspapers, followed by one or two emotive letters in their correspondence columns. Occasional articles, mostly describing the work of the NSPCC's newly-founded Battered Child Research Department, appeared in the press, and a few interested doctors published technical papers describing their findings. Dr Henry Kempe's work in Denver, Colorado, had caused widespread interest in the USA, but here the public at large continued to ignore a subject they apparently found too distressing to contemplate.

The Maria Colwell case has changed this picture entirely. There has been much public discussion on how and why it was that this child, known by her social workers, teachers and neighbours to be in danger, was returned to and allowed to remain in a potentially lethal home. However, although in the long run only good can come out of the increased public interest in the welfare of children, for the present this case has probably increased the already existing confusion between 'battering' and ordinary child abuse.

Maria was frequently referred to as a battered baby, but although it is true that William Kepple battered his stepdaughter to death, much of what is professionally implied by the phrase 'battered baby' was not present in this case. For one thing, Maria was badly neglected, and this is not normally a part of the 'battered child' syndrome. Chapter 2 will deal more fully with the distinction between them, but for the moment we may take it that 'child abuse' implies physical abuse suffered by a child of any age, while 'baby battering' narrows such abuse down to those injuries suffered by children, usually under

the age of four years, who have been attacked by their parents
or guardians who nevertheless appear genuinely anxious about
their welfare. Since a battered baby is also an abused baby, the
word 'abused' is occasionally used as a useful synonym for
'battered', particularly when 'battered' does not seem appropriate – for instance, where a burn is involved. Some people in
fact feel that 'battered baby' is too emotive and would like to
see the term dropped altogether. However, it remains a useful
aid in distinguishing a particular kind of child abuse.

In the majority of cases the children who have been battered can eventually be returned successfully to their homes.
Frequently their parents desperately want to make a happy
home for their family : their motivation is high and with sufficient knowledge and compassion they can be reached. Psychotic
and violently aggressive personalities on the other hand can
rarely be helped to the point where they will make satisfactory
parents, and this has to be accepted, particularly by the Juvenile
Courts who at present too frequently return children to parents
who are totally unsuited to bringing up children. Most baby
batterers, however, are emotionally immature people who expect too much from their children, who punish them too
severely for faults that in reality do not exist, but who nevertheless fuss over them, sometimes with over-protective fanaticism.
Neglected, starved children rarely fit into the technical category of 'baby battering' unless the mother is of such subnormal
intelligence or is so emotionally disturbed that she scarcely
knows what she is doing.

The main value of the Maria Colwell inquiry is that it has
brought some of the inadequacies of our present social system
to the notice of the general public. So much passionate interest
has been aroused that it is unlikely that the subject of child
abuse will entirely return to its previous obscurity. What must
not be allowed to happen, however, is for a scapegoat to be
found, allowing everyone to sit back in relief and turn their
minds to more pleasant subjects. No one person was to blame
for Maria's death, though bad misjudgements were certainly
made. The fault lies with our entire system of care for inade-

quate, overstressed families and for children known to be at risk.

Here and there are enlightened areas where a safety net is spread and maintained by groups of professionals – doctors, social workers, police – who willingly cooperate with each other. Unfortunately this situation is still comparatively rare: many tragedies occur because the various professionals involved distrust each other and will not work together, mainly because they look at battering from such different viewpoints. To one, even a case of mild battering is an atrocious crime deserving maximum punishment, while to another it is seen as the inevitable result of the bad 'mothering' the battering parent received in his or her own infancy, the pressing need being for sympathetic treatment, not punishment. The resulting problems of co-operation that face the social services, hospitals and the police are investigated in the following chapters, for until these differences are resolved there will continue to be tragedies which could have been averted. Every year between four and five thousand children are injured by their parents or guardians; it has been calculated that four hundred of these children under the age of one suffer permanent brain damage, many as a result of severe shaking (Ronald MacKeith). Probably as many as seven hundred children die annually. Not all of these could have been saved, however skilful the help available, but a great number could have been if enough help had been forthcoming.

When I began this book it was not the parents who progressed to killing their children who mainly interested me, but those parents who only just overstepped the line between smacking in a moment of temper, and actual battering. No one who has brought up children of their own can truthfully swear that never once have they ever felt like hitting their children really hard. At times, children can be exasperating, irritating and, perhaps worse, disappointing. Sometimes in our moments of anger all of us have slapped a little harder than we meant or shouted words we later regretted. But for most of us a short time of reflection is all we need to bring back our sense of balance. Perhaps we are able to recall that only the previous day we had laughed at the behaviour that had made us so angry today and we realize our anger was really caused by fatigue or some worry entirely unconnected with the child's misbehaviour.

What I wanted to find out was why some parents cannot put on the brakes as most parents do, why some parents who seem perfectly normal in most respects are able to hit their children so violently that limbs or even skulls are broken. Why was their breaking point so low, when by all accounts they loved their children, even rushing them to hospital for treatment for the very injuries they themselves had caused? Did they differ from ordinary people in some dramatic way or were they merely a little less stable, a little more stressed than the rest of us?

The first chapter of this book is the true story in her own words of a woman whose problems became unmanageable when her husband went blind. Mrs Jones, as we shall call her for the sake of anonymity, did not abuse her son very seriously. In most ways her story is typical of the kind of battering that goes on in thousands of homes all over the country. There are still many people who would prefer to imagine that it is only the odd monster who attacks his own child, but the truth is that if four or five thousand children are in fact seriously injured every year by their own parents, it is probable that many thousands more suffer mild attacks, most of which are not recognized as battering at all, even by the doctors or hospitals to whom these children are taken for treatment.

Later chapters will explore various aspects of more serious battering, but in terms of cumulative suffering it is the children who receive mild abuse whose cause most needs championing. They in their turn will grow up to be parents: like their own parents they cannot help but be inadequate, anxious, neurotic to some degree. Yet if they batter as they were battered, we shall blame them as though their failure were their own fault. Some of them will have been so emotionally injured as children that they will go further than their own parents and actually kill their children. But who is really to blame – them, or society?

It is time we stopped blaming, or excusing, or sympathizing in a woolly-minded way. It is time everyone worked together to break the cycle; even those of us with no professional involvement in child care can make certain that we keep up pressure on our MPs to improve the present conditions and to try to persuade the government to increase financial aid to the social services, the NSPCC and the hospitals. Even if the money will not be given for humanitarian reasons, is it not good economic sense to try to prevent a whole new generation of sick children from growing up and in their turn swelling the mental hospitals and the prisons? We cannot afford to go on as we are. The coming generation will have to overcome many problems if civilization as we know it is to survive: let us see that as many of them as possible are emotionally and physically equipped for the battle.

Chapter 1

A mother's story

When I was first introduced to Mrs Jones in 1973 I was surprised both by her apparent self-assurance and by her clothes. Knowing something of her story I had expected to see obvious signs of stress and even of poverty, but her miniskirt was freshly ironed and her long white boots were spotless in spite of the wet weather outside. Everything about her, from her careful make-up to the precise way she arranged her handbag and cigarettes on the table in front of her made it obvious she was a person who cared about order and propriety. Later, her health visitor told me she always dressed like that – it had not been a special effort to impress me. Her son Paul was invariably clean and tidy when he arrived at the clinic, and usually she would give a quick tug to his sweater or make a last-minute attempt to smoothe his naturally unruly hair. One of her regrets about Paul was that you cannot dress up boys the way you can girls.

Our first meeting was at her local clinic in a small room where the doctor saw the mothers. I deliberately chose for myself the chair where the mothers usually sit, giving Mrs Jones the doctor's seat; most battering parents cannot bring themselves to talk about what they have done so I did not want her to feel too conscious of being interviewed. I soon found out, though, that in this respect Mrs Jones was not at all typical. Not only was she very articulate but she was also anxious that other parents should benefit from her story. This readiness to talk freely had possibly saved Paul's life in the early days when she first began to attack him. It is true he is still at risk at the moment of writing, but it is unlikely she will physically attack him again, though his mental health is another matter altogether.

After several years of talking about herself to social workers and psychiatrists she was able to be open with me without any sign of embarrassment. She smoked cigarette after cigarette, but apart from that one sign of nervousness she might have been telling me about a new film she had seen. Until certain moments in the story, that is : then her voice rose a little and glimpses of the distraught woman beneath showed through. Determined to make everything as clear as she possibly could, she talked the whole morning, while in the room beyond the thin partition wall a group of small children played and sang under the direction of their nursery school teacher. One of the little boys was Paul, Mrs Jones's youngest child.

'I honestly haven't known anyone, really, who's had a baby like Paul. It's true I never did like boys, I've got this thing about them. I did think of having Paul adopted, but I couldn't go through with it. Paul wasn't my husband's child, you see.

'I was very much in love with the father (I still am, though I haven't seen him for four years) and Paul, he's the absolute image of his father, which is why I think he comes in for – you know, a lot of punishment from me. I look at him and I see Clive. Clive's his real father. It's uncanny, he's exactly the same to look at : his expression, his eyes.

'We were perfectly OK as a family until my husband Bill started going blind. His whole character changed then : he upset the entire family. He went completely impotent for one thing. The psychiatrist maintains he went like it at the shock of how he was told he was going to become blind. He wasn't built up, just told bluntly he was going to lose his sight in six months. He had laser beam treatment but it didn't work, so after a few months they sent him away for rehabilitation treatment. It wasn't explained to me it was the shock that made him impotent – I just thought he was going off me.

'Things got from bad to worse. There was a club we belonged to, and when it got he couldn't see so well, sometimes Clive used to ask me to dance, and we got friendly. By the time my husband was sent away I was longing for someone to – take an interest in me, and Clive sort of stepped in.

'I begged them not to send Bill away, I knew what would

happen because I'd already started getting some feelings towards Clive. Although he hadn't asked to see me outside the Club he used to sit and look, and I felt the same way. I asked if I could go with Bill and put the children into care, but they weren't very cooperative. Well, in the end he went. He was so eager to go.

'He'd been impotent for about six months before I found somebody else. While he was away his social worker, Mr Evans, came round. By then Clive was staying at the flat, and Mr Evans found out. He took it into his own hands to phone the rehabilitation centre where my husband was, to let him know. No, he didn't warn me what he was going to do. It was my health visitor who told me. She phoned me and said I think you ought to know your husband's on his way back home, and Mr Evans and myself are meeting the train at Paddington.

'It had been easy for Clive to stay at the flat, because he used to work at night. David and Wendy, they're my two oldest children, hardly ever saw him; he used to come after they'd gone to school and spend the day there, asleep most of the time. He got on very well with David and Wendy when he did see them: he was a nice man. I still miss him, you know, desperately.

'Anyway, my husband came back and there was a bit of a showdown. Clive had to move out quickly; I got him out of bed and packed his few things and he just got out in time. They all arrived, Mr Evans, the Child Officer, everyone, but instead of having a discussion about it Bill just pushed them all out of the door. He wouldn't let them stay and talk about it.

'So I left him: I collected a few clothes, got Wendy from school, and joined Clive. I still felt terribly sorry for Bill, though, even then. When I went I left David behind: he was only ten then, but Bill wasn't totally blind yet and he could still more or less cope.

'Altogether I was away for about three weeks. I used to ring up my sister, who was a sort of go-between, to make sure David was all right. One day she said to me, do you know they're going to have a court case about you? So I had to decide what to do next. They'd made up their minds to take me to court because

I was living with a man I wasn't married to, and as Wendy was with us, they thought she was in need of care. Also they thought my husband couldn't cope with David much longer.

'By then, I was pregnant. It was the second time. Yes, both of them Clive's. The first time I'd had an abortion: my husband swears to this day it was his child. He'd come back once for a weekend, and he tried to kid himself it was his. I didn't tell him different.

'I didn't mean to abort it. I went to the doctor's when I knew I was pregnant, and he called my husband in and said, well, your wife is pregnant, you don't want another child in your circumstances, do you? I panicked because I had visions of it not looking anything like the family at all, so I said no straight off. It was all arranged for me before I knew what was happening. The doctor phoned there and then to the hospital and arranged for me to see a psychiatrist; he told me what to do and I sort of fell in with it. Some people find it so hard to get an abortion, but for me it was so easy, it was all done for me. I went to see the psychiatrist and he said, Oh you don't want it, you're on the point of committing suicide, aren't you, so I said yes, like the doctor had told me to. I had it done when I was twelve weeks...I got pregnant again four months later. I had the abortion in September and by the New Year I was pregnant. I didn't take any precautions, I was determined to get pregnant again and have Clive's baby.

'Well, I didn't want to go back home when my sister told me about the court case, but I felt I had no choice. It was partly I felt sorry for him and partly because I wouldn't give Wendy up. I love Wendy very much and I won't part with her. We got on like a pair of sisters really. I used to hit David, but I never touched Wendy at all.

'No, I never hit David much, I don't suppose I hit him more than any other mother would probably, or perhaps just a bit harder. Like when he wet his trousers, I got really mad with him. And he was a bit slow starting at school. I used to sit and write his name for him to copy and things like that, and every time he got it wrong I used to hit him, I used to get so mad I'd hit him round the head. I felt he'd let me down, because people know me quite well locally. But I never touched Wendy.

'You see, I'd never had a good relationship with my own mother, I never remember kissing her : we weren't that sort of a family. Even when I got married I didn't kiss her or anything like that. So I wanted it to be different between me and my daughter. I shouldn't want to pass it down to Wendy – we're terribly close. I can't say I had any deep feelings for David but a lot of mothers are like that really; you can't help liking one a little bit more than the other sometimes.

'Anyway, in the end I decided to go back home and live with Bill, though Clive wanted me to stay with him. I felt mean, I felt I'd ruined his life. He wanted to marry me, and he really loved Wendy. But he couldn't get married, he was still getting a divorce, you see, because of someone before me, and it was taking such a long time. The authorities wouldn't let us have Wendy living with us.

'You know, once you get the authorities in you never get them out. They look at everything you do. Never a week goes past without there's somebody in our flat checking up. They think you'll think it's just a social visit – but it's not, you know what they're looking for. Once you're on their books! They keep having case conferences about our family, I think it's appalling: *it's wrong*! They call them without you knowing, they hold them behind your back and so many outsiders go to them. People you've never met before know you. You go in and there's a new doctor, and when you give your name they say, Oh, *hello* Mrs Jones! – just like that – and you know they know all about you. I mind it, I really do mind it. All sorts of people who've got no reason to know about me get told all the details – they sit in on conferences about me, that I know nothing about, and I'*m* not told about them. I don't think it's right. I feel I've no privacy left at all.

'I haven't got yet to the point where I sort of . . . hit Paul.

'Even after I'd gone back home to Bill I kept on seeing Clive for a while. I'd made an agreement with my husband that I would, because I couldn't bring myself to stop seeing Clive just like that. We agreed that I'd live at home but go twice a week to where Clive was living in the afternoon. That worked out OK for a while. Then we had a big row and my husband called me a whore and kicked me out. So I took Wendy – I left David with Bill – and began to live with Clive again.

'We went from hotel to hotel and I can't tell you how awful it was. Cheap hotels, you know; it was really awful. Then Wendy got the 'flu so I went home again. It had only lasted about three weeks, that's all. I had to stay at home after that because I was feeling so rotten with my pregnancy, but I carried on seeing him for a little while. But in the end I said to him, it's not fair to you, going on like this, and it's not fair to me; we've got to decide one way or the other. He wanted me to live with him and get married when his divorce came through, but I said how can we, how are we going to find a flat with two children? So we just said goodbye, and I haven't seen him since.

'I still look out for him, even now, four years after.

'When Paul was born they didn't show him to me because my records said I was going to have him adopted. I had to do that because I'd already got rid of what Bill still thought of as his baby, so obviously the decent thing for me to do was to have Clive's child adopted. Deep down, I knew I wouldn't go through with it. But when I had Paul they didn't even say it was a boy, they just whisked it away, sort of picked him up and put him over the back of me, and I didn't see him till I asked what sex it was.

'I was terribly disappointed when they told me. I just don't like boys all that much. You can't even dress them up like you can girls. I never liked boys. My father always worshipped boys, and my brothers always had preference at home. Even now, my father'll give a pound, say, to David on his birthday and fifty pence to Wendy, which is wrong, isn't it? And at Christmas David always gets an extra present than Wendy. At home – in my parents' home, that is – they've got several photos on the sideboard of my two brothers, but there aren't any of me and my sisters, not one. My eldest sister, I think *she* could have been classed as a battered child, though you didn't have them then, did you? The rest of us weren't hit like that, though. I suppose it's brushed off a bit onto David, and now Paul. . .

'They were a bit offhand with me in the nursing home, because of the adoption thing; they'd been very nice to me when I'd had the other two there.

'It started as soon as I got home. They'd got me a home help but she wasn't very good. The trouble was she was only partially sighted herself. She did her best, I suppose, but she just came in and put the duster round, and I wanted someone who could cook a meal or do something in the home, do a bit of washing for me. Then I got phlebitis again which always happens after I've had a baby. Another thing, they didn't tell me in the hospital what they were feeding him on – I decided not to breast-feed him – so I didn't know what to give him. It was like having a first baby again. It was an eight year gap, you see, and that's a long time. He wasn't painful to give birth to, I had natural childbirth, but I was terribly ill carrying him. I kept fainting. They thought he must be lying on a nerve which was cutting off oxygen to the brain. I kept being carted off to different hospitals because I was always passing out in the road.

'I keep putting it off, don't I, about Paul. I tell you, when I hear about a mother who's battered her child, I sympathize, I really do. Because Paul so *nearly* became a battered baby – he was just on the borderline – and if I hadn't been lucky enough to have a good person at the Welfare. . .

'I got so desperate with Paul. I remember meeting a health visitor out in the street – I wasn't under her – and she said, hello, you've had your baby? I said yes. I said, if only he'd sleep, he hasn't slept since I've had him – he was about two months then – I hadn't had one night's sleep, and that meant every two hours he'd wake, every two hours! And I'd do everything I knew. I'd feed him, I'd change him and give him extra food, and still he wouldn't sleep. I was so desperate. "Oh, he'll settle down, in three months he'll settle, he'll change at three months."

'I waited for three months to come, he didn't change, he went on and on, and every week, twice a week, I was round at the clinic, and in the end they must have thought I was something odd! I'd walk in there and they'd look at one another as though to say, well here she comes again about her baby. But they didn't know how desperate I was. They don't understand. One time I was so tired, they said give him a dummy, it doesn't matter what people say – so I gave him a dummy. Sometimes I'd shove my hand really hard over his mouth with the dummy in it to try to stop him crying.

'I'd take him into bed with me to try to stop him but he went on crying. He was still crying three or four times a night when he was twelve months, and still they hadn't done anything. Then this time, I just got hold of him, I threw him to the bottom of the bed, I was so . . . of course things between my husband and myself were so bad I mean. . . I threw him really hard, but I suppose fortunately for Paul he hit the wooden bit at the bottom of the bed and didn't fall off. Of course he came up with a lovely big bruise, all his eye was cut and bruised.

'I didn't think too much of it, I put a dressing on it and took him to the clinic as usual a couple of days later. When I put him on the scales the nurse said, "Oooh, how'd he get that, Mrs Jones?" and I told her, I said he'd driven me absolutely mad, worse than usual. I'd had enough, I said, so I just threw him out of bed. Next thing I knew the senior health visitor came out of her office and said, "Hello, Mrs Jones, having trouble with Paul?" I said, "Well, you know I am, I've been having trouble with him ever since he was born." She said, "What happened to him?" I told her I threw him out of bed and said, "You would have done it too." I warned them I'd do it again; it wouldn't have stopped at that. I was honest with them.

'They sort of stepped in from there. They said, "Let's make an appointment with this paediatrician at the – Hospital, he's very good, he'll get him to sleep"; so I said, "All right." The health visitor was very kind, she came and picked me up in the car and I thought this is good. I thought it was funny, though, the paediatrician just asked me a few questions, like did I love Paul. I said, "I suppose so." I told him he wasn't my husband's child because he asked if everything was going well at home. Then he said he was going to get him X-rayed. I asked him what for, and he said just to see his bones are all right; perhaps he's got something not growing properly which makes him wake up in the middle of the night crying. But it wasn't for that, it was to see whether I'd been battering him.

'They X-rayed him from top to bottom – did he scream! I had to hold him because he was rigid and screaming. They asked me if I would hit him again and I said, "Yes, I would." After that I had to fight like mad for them not to keep him there and then at the hospital (they said it was just to give me a few days' rest) because something in my mind ticked over that once they got him they'd keep him.

'They all had a case conference about me later. There was an inspector from the NSPCC, the doctor from the clinic and Bill's social worker, Mr Evans. They wanted to take Paul from me, but Dr — said no, I wasn't the sort of mother who would really bash a baby (Mr Evans told me this afterwards), it was the circumstances which made me do these things, so they let me have him back. They made me go to a psychiatrist, though, and I've been under her ever since, but it's not compulsory any more now. She said it's deeper, it's not just Paul's sleeping problems, it's all the family relationships. She's tried to get the problems between my husband and myself sorted out. I only feel safe now when I go up there once a week, because I could still hurt Paul, I know I could.

'I burned him later with the iron; I did it deliberately. I'd look at him, and think, oh you little bastard, you know? I just got hold of him and burned him on the back of the hand. I was so fed up! He'd been grizzling; he was tired out in the daytime because he didn't sleep at night. And of course *I* was tired too, and he wouldn't stop grizzling. I was ironing on the floor in the lounge because it was just something quick I wanted – I was kneeling down and he was sitting over by the window. I just got hold of his hand and I said, *that'll* make you sleep! It was all done in such a quick second, you know, that I didn't . . . it wasn't sort of premeditated; I just looked at him, had the iron in my hand, and did it. I took him round to the health visitor the same day, and I said, Paul's burned his hand. She said, just a minute, I'll dress it for you (it had come up in a blister). When she came back she said to me, "Why did you do it?"

'They decided they'd take Paul into the day nursery to get him away from me, and for me to have a break. He was about fifteen months by then. It did help a lot. I only had to pick up the iron after that when he went to bed. He was terrified of that iron – he would scream and I got a lot of satisfaction out of him screaming. If he cried in the middle of the night I'd show him the iron – it wasn't heated up or anything and he used to scream like mad. It didn't stop him crying but . . . I got satisfaction. That sounds terrible, but it's true.

'You see, having my husband there as well: *he's* like a child. But poor Paul, he's going to suffer the whole time. I said to Mrs Morris my health visitor the other day, the outcome of this family episode is going to be one of two things: I'm either going to walk out and sort of disappear, or I'm going to take Paul and jump off the bridge or something.

'Yes, I did try to commit suicide once . . . I felt so terrible. That was an awful Thursday. My psychiatrist was there and she phoned up a hospital – a place where families with problems like ours can go and stay – and they sent two nurses down.

'I tell you something I find: if you're a married woman, you don't get the right sort of help. I desperately wanted someone in the home to help me, because I couldn't get organized or anything. For four years now they've talked about sending Paul and myself away, just for a break, or sending my husband away – they talk about it, but nobody ever does anything: they're going to wait until I do something desperate.

'If only they hadn't brought back my husband unexpected that time, if it had all been done some other way, perhaps I could still be seeing Paul's father; *I'd* be happy and I wouldn't resent my husband for having no sex. Because I never did see Clive again, not after that last time I told you about. He kept driving by but he never went to the club any more.

'There was just one time when I talked to him. Only talked, I didn't see him. We'd moved: they got us a flat in a new tower block – fifteen floors up – it's a bit isolated. In those days the intercom telephone still worked and one day it rang. I went out onto the landing to answer it, and it was Clive. He said, "Hello, it's Clive here. You've had the baby by now, what was it?" My husband was beside me, he follows me round like a shadow, so I said, "It's a boy, but it's no business of yours." I said, "If you come round again I'll call the police, I don't want anything to do with you." He kept on saying he wanted to see it, but I said, "No, it's nothing to do with you at all." I just *had* to say that, what else could I say with my husband standing there beside me? Had Bill been out, though, I'd have let Clive in, and it would have started up again, I know it would.

'I'd like him to see Paul, just once. . . I'm so proud of Paul in a sort of way, he's a nice-looking boy.

'But if only he'd sleep. You won't believe it, but even now he still comes into bed every night. I still haven't had a night's sleep with Paul. He's been on a sleeping mixture for two years : the psychiatrist gives it to me but she won't let me have more than about twelve days' supply. The dose used to be one teaspoon, but he's immune to it now so he has two. Sometimes I've given him a double dose even of that and still he'll wake up. He comes in every night between two and three and he'll say, "Hello mummy", and I'll say, "Get in." They used to tell me to take him back when he first started doing it. It's easy enough for doctor to sit there and say, take him back; but when you're so tired because it's gone on for so long, how can you get out in the middle of the night, knowing after you get back he'll still be crying behind you – you can't do it, you're so tired you just say, get into bed then. I think it would do people good – child guidance people, doctors, all of them – if they had the child to live with them, to see exactly what it was like, and how they'd feel after a month of it. My psychiatrist says I'm tense and unhappy, and I'm conveying it to Paul. Well, *of course* I am, how can I help it? Lots of people think you exaggerate, but they honestly don't know what it's like. They can't know. And when I read in the paper of a child being battered I don't say, "Poor kid," I say, "Oh poor woman, what she's gone through."

'Did I mean to kill myself? Yes, I think so, I think I really meant to do it. I was in a very bad state. I went to my own doctor to get some strong sleeping pills but he wasn't terribly sympathetic. He just said it was my nerves, and gave me something very mild. So I told my psychiatrist that I needed to get a good night's sleep and I wanted some strong pills. She said no – I think she sensed what was in my mind – no, wait and see how you feel next week. Then on Thursday morning my husband and I had the usual row about what I am – a whore, I keep getting that, I shall always have it, I suppose. Paul had already gone to the nursery. I knew my psychiatrist would be at the hospital so I went up there and asked to see her. They let me go in front of several people and I told her I had to have some sleeping pills. She said no again, and I sort of broke down then, and cried. So she said, "Look, I think you ought to come in for a couple of nights' good rest; we'll take care of Paul and after that you'll feel different." She put me in a little room while she went off to get me admitted. I waited for two or three minutes, then I thought, *no*! – I had this great thing they were going to take Paul away from me : I won't let anyone take Paul away, I'd rather do away with him, I won't let anybody take him from me! So I rushed out of the hospital to the road.

'It's a very busy road, very difficult to get across. I saw her coming, there were two of them looking for me, and I tried to get under a car, but there was an ambulance parked near by and one of the ambulance men jumped out and the psychiatrist, all of them, they sort of sensed what I was going to do. I don't know very much what happened then : the three of them grabbed me and I was back on the pavement and she said, we're going to have to admit you. I don't know to this day how I got away from her but I did; between the wings of the hospital there are a lot of gardens and it's quite easy to disappear. Then I got a taxi to the nursery here. I saw matron and said Paul had a hospital appointment I'd forgotten about, so she let me have him.

'I roamed about after that, not knowing what to do, whether to go under a bus or not : it was awful, it went on for hours, me just walking about holding Paul, not knowing where to go or what to do. In the end Paul started crying because he was hungry, so eventually I went back home. When I got there, there was my psychiatrist in a great state looking for me; Mrs Morris my health visitor was there, and Mr Evans; the vicar was there: everyone. Later these two nurses from the residential hospital turned up, and waiting across the road in the pub in case she was needed was the Chief Child Welfare Officer – she's the one who can authorize the child to be taken away if she decides it's really in danger – and there was somebody else with her as well. All these people were on hand in case they wanted me put away! The psychiatrist kept on saying to me, "Are you going to try and do it again?" I said, "I don't know, I might, I don't know."

'They wanted me to go away with Paul to hospital but I wouldn't. They couldn't force me, I wasn't barmy enough for that. But in spite of the fact that I refused to go, really I wish they'd made me. Underneath it I really wanted to go.

'It was like other times when I kept trying to tell them how desperate I was. If only they'd said to me, you've got to go away for a week with Paul, no ifs or buts. Psychiatrists are the same, all they do is talk, they never come up with any solution. I'm no nearer now to a solution (I don't think there is one) than I was four years ago.

'One of the reasons I didn't want to go away was that I couldn't have taken Wendy and I didn't dare leave her at home with my husband for the simple reason she'd already said she'd run away if I ever did. And she would have done, too.

'Well, there we are; that's about it. We don't really live together as a family any more. There's this terrible atmosphere. My husband hardly talks to my daughter; they fight like cat and dog and I have to go and separate them. Wendy's only twelve, it's a very emotional age and all this is going to have an effect on her. They wanted David to go to child guidance but after a couple of times he stopped going. He's fourteen now so I can't make him go if he doesn't want to. It's not surprising he's all mixed up when there's so much tension in the house. Bill and I hardly ever speak to each other, they never see him put his arm round me for a cuddle or anything. I haven't even kissed him for four years. We all play one up against the other, it's so awful.

'Money problems make it worse. We used to work together in a little printing shop before he got ill. He was the boss at work and I was the boss at home, and it worked out very well, we were ever so happy. In those days we used to have two wage packets; now we're living on Social Security. I have to ask for grants for clothes and things like that; it's very degrading when you've not been used to it.

'I'd go out to work now if I could, but they'd deduct all but about £2 of my money and it wouldn't be worth all the organizing I'd have to do. You just can't manage on Social Security, not when you've been used to a certain standard of living; they don't realize that, and they won't let you earn more. Last week I had to ask the social worker for some money for shoes for David : you have to go and ask, you see, they never ask *you* if you want anything — you don't get a clothing grant or anything like that. I very rarely ask because unless you're prepared to go and sit up there and cry in front of them and say you've got nothing, etc., etc., you don't get given anything. I mostly rely on cast-offs; neighbours are very good. I hate to crawl.

'They come to your home to check on you, you know. I always keep it clean and tidy and we had quite a good home before this happened; we've got furniture and a nice radiogram and things like that still, so they think we're all right and don't really need anything. But we do; sheets don't last for ever and things wear out all the time. They just don't seem to realize that if you manage to make things look nice in spite of it all. . .

'It's not only money, though : it's Bill. Since Bill went blind he's changed so much. It's been like living with a different man. Mr Evans, Bill's social worker, doesn't help much, he's not even fully trained. He's the one who told Bill about Clive and me that time when Bill was away at the rehabilitation centre. He comes every week, sits down with a cup of coffee like a member of the family and we talk about general things, but the problem he really comes for we never discuss. Yes, I suppose I've more or less forgotten about him telling Bill, but I can't say I like him. I never will. He's not at all like my Mrs Morris.

'What it comes down to is I've got this need to punish some-one. I can't punish my husband because – it doesn't matter what I do – he still loves me so much. But he just sits in that armchair until I could scream. He does these flints as homework for a bit of cash. You hear this click click click – a grown man! He won't go out to the centre because it's only for mentally handicapped people and my husband's not mental. It's supposed to cover physical but there's more mental than physical and my husband won't go because he said he'll become like one of them, which is probably true. If only they got him out of the house every morning it would make him more of a man, he'd get his manhood back again. He doesn't get any exercise, and I won't take him out now because he won't make the effort to go out by himself – he was trained but he won't go. He doesn't really accept he's blind : he hasn't adjusted, I think.

'One thing, him being at home like that has meant he's had more to do with Paul than the others. He's brought Paul up, he's given him his bottle, nursed him for hours on end as a baby. They're so close, I think he's brainwashed himself into thinking Paul's his son, you know? He says to me, "You'll touch him over my dead body," or things like "I'll tell him what you're really like." And that really gets me going, because he's not *his* child, he's *mine*. He's mine only, he's not even his real father's now. I regard Paul as *my* property and nobody's going to have Paul. He's the only thing I've got left of Clive, and if I thought my husband . . . well, he *is*, he's winning him away from me.

'It'll be like it was with David. David's caused a lot of rows because my husband has always defended him. Underneath, deep down, I suppose I love David, I try to treat them all fairly. If I give Wendy money, David gets the same. He's not doing well at school because he's unhappy – it's a shame, he's got a high IQ. He's terribly embarrassed about my husband's blindness. He won't go out with him, take him anywhere. I honestly can't remember when I last kissed David – years and years ago.

Wendy, now, she can't sleep unless I go in and kiss her. But David, I hit him, I punch him and he fights me back. He's as big as I am now, broader, but I have to hit him, he swears like a trooper at me.

'The thing I'm so worried about is that it's going to be twice as bad with Paul, because he's not my husband's child and I resent him more already than I ever did David. I love him – I don't want to be parted from him – but every time I look at him I see his father and think of what I've given up and all the problems at home, the stress.

'I'm not a very religious person but I go to church practically every Sunday and that makes me feel guilty because if I believe in the Church I shouldn't act this way to Paul. I hate myself. I feel sorry I've had Paul; he didn't ask to be born – I wanted Clive's child and I was just unlucky enough to get a boy : with a girl I don't think it would have happened. Deep down I love Paul, but I just can't help these feelings. It's the same with my husband : I hate him but I must love him in a way, though I hardly know if it's love or pity now.

'Lately Paul's been getting very vicious, and my husband says it's a brush-off from me to him. Wendy will be sitting down and Paul'll come up and punch her. She gets upset and starts crying so I go for Paul. My husband tries to rush to get him before I do, because he knows that I really will wallop him and perhaps throw him across the room. And then it starts. The neighbours must love it, they must all turn their television sets down and have a good listen. And yet every time I hit Paul he'll come back and he'll love me and I'll cuddle him and kiss him.

'I punish him more mentally now. The nurses, they're very sweet but they're very fly, and if they see a mark on him they're going to jump. Even though I think they like me and they understand my problems, they're going to jump for Paul's sake. So I punish him mentally. It's cruel, I know it is. What sort of thing? Well, sometimes I tell him I don't love him, or I try and frighten him. If he comes to get on my lap I push him off. It's such a pity, he's a lovely boy really, and he's so affectionate. If *only* they'd do something. All they do is talk; they'll never act until I maim Paul. But I don't hit him any more so he's marked, I'm too clever for that now.

'Oh, yes, he's had quite a lot of little bruises in the past, but nothing else as bad as those two times. Sometimes I'd hit him or push him so he'd fall against the door. I knew what I was doing. I used to throw him across the room a lot, too, as a toddler. Or if I was going out of a room and he got in the way, happened to toddle or crawl in front of me, instead of me saying as another mother would, "Out of my way, Tinker," I wouldn't, I'd just boot him one out of the way.

'I don't *mean* to do it, that's the thing, I'm not that sort of person. I'm not a cruel person. In fact I regard myself as very lucky, because I know what I *could* do, and the fact that I'm so deep in with the authorities means that they're keeping an eye on Paul for me. What helps most of all is having him out of the house at the nursery from 9.30 until teatime.

'Not long ago I kept him at home because he said he'd tell matron that I'd hit him (he has bronchitis so it's easy to get away with keeping him at home). But he got on my nerves so much! For one thing, he won't eat his dinner for *me* but he eats it at the nursery, though I give him the same things. I find out what he has there but he won't eat it for me. I get so cross I just pick up the plate and throw the stuff in the sink and it's gone, whether or not he's hungry.

'There's another thing that frightens me; it won't be long now before I'm forty. When you start expecting the change you're bound to get more emotional. I know at different times of the month already Paul comes in for it. Just before, *you know*, I'm so tense and worked up I scream and shout, and I'm not placid at all; usually I'm quite a placid person. Paul comes in for more pushes and hits then than at any other time. All women are like that.

'And again, getting older means I haven't too many years left when I'm sexually attractive to other men. I've lost four years, and I'm getting rather desperate in myself, and the more desperate I get the more it's going to come out onto Paul, because he's the only person I can hurt.

'It really drives me mad; my husband and I sleep in a double bed together and that's all that's happened for four years. We get into bed, just literally *say* goodnight. I turn over my way and he turns over his. People have got to do it for four years to believe what it's like. I've not been out with anyone since Paul's father. I get too involved, I can't just go out and have a quickie with a man – I'm not that sort. I think a man can, but a woman gets more emotionally involved; it's deeper with a woman.

'I keep saying I'm going to get a man, but it's so difficult: living in a tower block you can't get away with a thing. Anyway, just to do it three or four times, and all those sneaky . . . it's not the same. I used to feel bad enough when I was going out twice a week to see Paul's father. My husband would be waiting for me – he knew what I'd been doing. I'd open the door and walk in, and for your husband to know you've been sleeping with your boyfriend, it's awful. Sometimes if it was in the evening he'd be waiting up and as soon as I'd put the key in the door he'd make a cup of coffee or get the cups ready, and we'd just pretend that I hadn't been anywhere.

'I feel I'm odd living with a man and not sleeping with him. Every other week we're going to separate, we have great quarrels, but afterwards he says to me, it's all blown over now, hasn't it, and I say, oh yes, I suppose so. I talk about it all to the psychiatrist, she's very sweet, but nothing's done materially, you know? I've had three years of it now – we talk for half an hour and it's hopeless really, but I keep going up there because I feel safe, and it's someone to talk to. If I was cut off altogether from her and Mrs Morris, I'd think Paul would come in for a lot more bashing.

'The social workers and that, they're interested in you but they don't *do* anything until something desperate happens. When there's a crisis, it's different, then you get everybody. Then they *love* it. Mr Evans is never happier than when there's a real crisis in the family; they all thrive on crises, social workers.

'I wonder whether a person's right to try and struggle on

and not break, not have a breakdown? I've been so near it so many times. It's only sheer will-power that's kept me going. I think you're better off to have one, I think you must emerge as a different person, perhaps : until you've had one, you don't know.

'Now that it's mental cruelty with Paul, the psychiatrist says she'd rather I gave him a good hitting than keep up this sort of cold war I'm having with him. But I didn't mean it to be like that at all. I wanted it to be so different. I wanted to get married and have children of my own. I imagined David would go out in the evening with his girl-friend and say, "Goodbye, Mum," and give me a kiss. I thought we were going to be such a nice close-knit family, just the sort of atmosphere I didn't have at home. I don't mean you've got to keep kissing all the time, but I did think we'd be such an intimate sort of family.

'I don't know what the end of it all will be, I really don't know. Something's going to happen, but I don't know what.'

Chapter 2

What is baby battering?

My reactions to hearing Mrs Jones's story were different from what I had imagined they would be. I had not expected to feel so sympathetic towards a mother who had treated her own child as she had Paul. At the same time her reasonableness and her obvious honesty made her treatment of him the more shocking. How could such a woman deliberately burn her own child, and then later threaten him with the same iron?

The word 'deliberately' is introduced intentionally, because it is the kind of word that judges use in their summings-up, and, with the full weight of the law behind it, it has a very callous ring. By using the word 'deliberately', I am implying only that Mrs Jones knew what she was doing: she did not have a black-out nor was she swept away by passion. But she certainly did not sit down and *deliberate* or work out what she was going to do: as she herself said, 'It was all done in such a quick second, you know, that I didn't . . . it wasn't sort of premeditated.'

It is fatally easy to make a mental progression from the first meaning to the second, particularly in reading legal reports, and what little sympathy we might have with battering parents may be dissipated through a misinterpretation of a common word. This point is stressed because it is important to be as free from prejudice as possible when reading about this emotionally heated subject.

With Mrs Jones's story we are immediately faced with one particularly difficult hurdle: for most people it is less easy to accept that a mother can burn a loved child than to accept that she could hit it. I have tried unsuccessfully to persuade several doctors and psychologists to define a personality difference between parents who hit and those who burn, but the general feeling is that the actual form of injury is purely a question of the parent's own particular fears or inhibitions, and is not relevant beyond that. To one mother screaming uncontrollably and/or flinging a child against a wall is the ultimate, while for another, burning is. So we must look beyond our own personal reactions to the particular *kind* of punishment a parent actually inflicts, to consider instead the *degree* to which he inflicts it.

Clearly there is a world of difference between a father who occasionally loses his temper to the point where he hits his son hard enough to knock him down, and a father who repeatedly beats his child until the boy is a mass of bruises and half-healed fractures. The first father might more or less accidentally cause a fracture; the second father might eventually kill his child. In the light of really violent cases, Mrs Jones's attacks were very mild indeed. The mental suffering she has caused Paul will probably prove more harmful in the long run, as her own psychiatrist has pointed out to her.

What is the precise meaning of battering if it does not simply mean that a baby has been picked up and battered? If it can only be a parent figure who is involved, how are we to distinguish between an excess of parental strictness and the first stages of battering? At the other extreme, what is the difference between an insane psychotic who brutally murders his child in an uncontrollable attack, and a parent who repeatedly abuses his child until eventually it dies? There can be no simple answer, since we are not dealing with an inert substance which can be scientifically evaluated, but with live people who rarely fit neatly into any precise slot. After all, the phrase 'battered child' itself did not even come into existence until 1961.

The phrase was Dr Henry Kempe's. Dr Kempe, an eminent American paediatrician, had grown increasingly concerned at the large numbers of children who were brought to his clinic suffering from injuries which were clearly not accidental. There was no satisfactory way of explaining these injuries unless the possibility that their own parents had caused them was taken into account. But there was still a great deal of resistance to that idea.

Battering, of course, is no new phenomenon. Children have always been abused by their parents, but because such medical aids as X-rays were not available until comparatively recently, many symptoms were not recognized as having been caused by physical abuse. Rickets, syphilis, malnutrition, scurvy, fragile bones : many explanations were given to explain away swellings caused by fractures. Several children in one family suffering from such problems only confirmed the diagnosis instead of causing suspicion. The discovery of X-rays in 1895 opened the way to greatly improved diagnoses, although the newly-revealed injuries to the bones of infants thoroughly puzzled doctors, who at first could find no clinical reason for them.

Medical papers suggesting various diagnoses began to be published and gradually further pieces of the jigsaw began to fit together. In 1946 the real breakthrough came when John Caffey, an American radiologist, described six cases where fractures to the bones of young infants were accompanied by subdural haematoma (blood clots under the skull). He suggested that these injuries had a violent origin and were not caused by a natural weakness or illness. In 1953 Dr Silverman, another eminent American radiologist, insisted that such children had definitely been attacked, and this view was finally confirmed by Drs Woolley and Evans in 1955 after an eight-year study of injured children and their parents.

However, most people still found difficulty in accepting the possibility that parents could be responsible for battering their own children. It was not until 1961 when Dr Kempe, directing a symposium conducted by the American Academy of Pediatrics, used the deliberately emotive phrase 'battered child syndrome' that the subject became really widely discussed. The resultant publicity revolutionized attitudes everywhere : many doctors and social workers throughout the world followed Dr Kempe's lead and began to look more closely at the young children coming to them with injuries which were somehow puzzling.

One important fact to emerge was that the newly-defined battered children were rarely found to be neglected; indeed, it is generally accepted that one easily recognizable symptom of a battering mentality is an excessive concern with neatness or cleanliness. The child must at all costs be a credit to his parents.

What are the differences between neglect, abuse and batter-ing? A *neglected* child might be undernourished, insufficiently clothed, perhaps left unattended for hours at a time or even all night. He may never be physically attacked in any way but he is likely to suffer various accidents because nobody thinks to remove dangers out of his way. There may be real love between him and his family, or there may be absolute indifference on the part of the parents – either way, the child's welfare is neglected. The physical *abuse* of children has been defined by Dr D. Gil (in Helfer and Kempe [eds.], *The Battered Child*, 1968) as 'non-accidental physical attack or physical injury, including minimal as well as fatal injury, inflicted upon children by per-sons caring for them'. Again, the quality of the parents' affection for their child is not relevant to the diagnosis of 'abuse'. A *battered* baby is a baby who is also physically abused by his parents or guardians, and whose injuries are often repeated. Nevertheless, his parents, who appear to love him, are generally over-fussy, over-anxious and over-possessive.

Mrs Jones may serve as an example: 'I had this great thing they were going to take Paul away from me: I won't let any-one take Paul away, I'd rather do away with him'; and again later, when discussing her husband's relationship with Paul, 'He's not *his* child, he's *mine*. He's mine only, he's not even his real father's now. I regard Paul as *my* property.' Her possessive-ness is not very attractive, but her love for the boy is clear, in spite of the problems he has brought her. As she says, 'I love him – I don't want to be parted from him – but every time I look at him I see his father and think of what I've given up and all the problems at home, the stress.'

One psychiatric theory is that battering one's child is only another way of punishing one's own flesh. When Mrs Jones punishes Paul she is punishing herself, not only for her guilt over the pain she knows she has caused her husband but also for what she sometimes sees as her own weakness in not walk-ing out on him to go to Clive, the man she really loved. Paul's unfortunate resemblance to his real father only increases her ambivalence between love and hate for him: he is a thorn in her side reminding her all the time of the lover she has lost. Again, although she is drawn to him by the very fact of this resemblance, her upbringing has taught her to distrust and dislike boys. She can never quite put out of her mind her life-long jealousy of her brothers.

The term 'battered baby' is becoming more common than 'battered child' probably because most infants are battered at a surprisingly early age. In the NSPCC's *Study of Suspected Child Abuse* (1972) 19 per cent of the babies were five months old or under, 18 per cent were between six and eleven months, 14 per cent were between twelve and seventeen months and 11 per cent between eighteen and twenty-three months, making a total of 62 per cent being attacked under two years of age. The figures in their earlier 1969 *Retrospective Study* were even more startling: 56 per cent of the babies were under twelve months and 22 per cent between one and two years of age. After about four years of age the pattern usually changes for various reasons. Paul, for example, is now able to hold off his mother's attacks by threatening to tell the matron of his nursery school. Also, at the hospital, the older child can contradict his parents' explanations.

The discrepancies between the parents' explanation of the child's injuries and the actual injuries is one of the ways that battering is now recognized. The sister in charge of the children's ward of a large London hospital defined battering to me as a case of abuse where the injuries are inconsistent with the explanation of the accident given by the parent. She added, 'Children bounce. Recently we had in a child who'd fallen nearly fifty feet from a building and it hadn't even fractured its skull. But another mother brought in her baby with a severe injury which can only have been caused by an attack, and do you know what her explanation was? It had fallen off the table!' This particular sister was worrried that publicity about battered babies might make parents reluctant to bring in children suffering from genuine accidents, in case they were suspected of having hurt the child themselves. She emphasized that an experienced staff could nearly always tell immediately whether or not an explanation was the correct one.

We have now looked at several definitions of baby battering – battered children are normally under four years of age, and most frequently are under two; they are very rarely neglected but are rather the victims of over-anxious, over-possessive parents; they have been attacked by those who are supposed to be caring for them (i.e. an intruder burgling a house and assaulting a child is by definition not a baby batterer); often the batterer punishes the child as though he were punishing himself (this aspect will be looked at in greater detail later); and finally, after some delay, the parents usually take the child for medical attention but betray themselves by giving unlikely explanations for the injuries.

To clarify the situation even further, here are some descriptions of battering by three people who have been deeply concerned with the problem. First is Joan Court, the original head of the NSPCC Battered Child Research Department. She wrote : 'Battering is a potentially lethal disease and a significant cause of infant deaths and morbidity in many countries.' Looked at as a disease it becomes considerably easier to see the parents not as sadists to be shunned but as sick people suffering from a literally killing illness. Infected themselves in their infancy, they pass on their sickness to their surviving children, who in turn perpetuate this terrible disease unless at some point the chain is broken. Mrs Jones's own sister was battered and she herself was clearly emotionally deprived : what kind of parents will her own three children grow up to be?

The next two comments come from men with very different views. The first was made by a consultant paediatrician :

The fact of the matter is, this is not a crime like others : it's not like hitting someone over the head to take their purse. No standard criminal gets a three months old baby and bashes its head then takes the evidence to show what they'd done to authority. If you bash someone on the head you run away and leave them to die on the street, you don't pick up the victim and take him to the nearest hospital, which is exactly what these parents do.'

On the other hand Detective Superintendent Roy of North-ampton, one of the founders of an excellent scheme for over-coming the problems of liaison between the various authorities who deal with battering parents, sees battering as essentially a crime.

You mustn't divorce this from other sorts of crime – when you talk about battered babies, by definition you're talking about children against whom criminal offences have been committed. Battering is an offence under Section 47 of the Offences against the Person Act, actual bodily harm. . . Let's be sensible about this : is there any difference between a distraught young mother who batters her child, and a distraught daughter looking after an aged mother who batters that aged mother?

Finally here is a brief passage taken from Juliet Berry's *Social Work with Children*. She writes : 'I have an image of a batter-ing mother combing her child's hair with harsh thoroughness, whereas a neglecting mother may not even bother to comb her own hair'. It does not take much imagination to see how short a step it is from tugging a brush through the tangled hair of a resisting child to clouting that child round the head with the brush when she tries to escape once too often : what parent's fingers have not itched to do just that in similar circumstances? Battering often takes place while the infant is being attended to : a resisting child can be particularly irritating, especially if the mother has been deprived of sleep, as is very often the case. Time and time again battering parents report sleeping problems, and no one consistently deprived of their proper quota of sleep can be said to be fully themselves. Add this to their other prob-lems, and their actions begin to seem more comprehensible and therefore less horrifying.

Even now, more than a decade after Kempe's first use of the phrase, there are still people who deny that defining a battered baby as such has any use. An abused child is an abused child, and that's all there is to it, they say. Others feel that battering is receiving far too much attention : only a small fraction of children coming under care have been battered, and they do not want to see scarce resources concentrated on one small field of child care to the possible exclusion of the rest. Most important of all is the fact that there are still many people – doctors, lawyers and social workers among them – who deny that battering, as it has been defined, exists at all. They cannot bring themselves to accept that 'ordinary' people could ever attack their own children. 'Pathological', 'insane monster', are the kinds of words thrown around by people who ought to know better, as though battering parents can be brushed out of existence by denying their customary normality. Certainly they are sick but they are not insane, nor are they monsters (though it is true that when coming across severe cases it is difficult, even for those who deal regularly and sympathetically with battering parents, to feel anything at first other than revulsion for the attacker). But these extreme cases must not be allowed to deflect care and sympathy away from the more common type of battering parent who can nearly always be successfully helped.

It is not easy for a family doctor to bring himself to suspect that a patient, whom he may have known for many years, has attacked her own child. Some doctors frequently accept explanations which are patently untrue without making any further inquiries. For example, one paediatrician told me about a little girl he had recently been treating. 'She had already been treated earlier by another hospital – not this one – for a head injury, but they'd done nothing formal about it. I doubt if anyone at all realized at that time what had actually happened. When she was admitted here with this second head injury we did some investigating and naturally got suspicious when we discovered that the mother had been attending a psychiatrist for some time. It turned out she was very depressed, a totally immature and incompetent personality, with three children under five. She couldn't cope with it all, it was beyond her. It was a professional family, quite well off in their late twenties. Now my point here is that their doctor, a personal friend of theirs by the way, simply did not realize what had been happening. He *wouldn't* realize it, absolutely refused to. When we rang him and suggested there was a possibility the child had been battered he nearly jumped down our throats. . .'

If that family doctor had been able to accept the possibility earlier that a pleasant, middle-class woman whom he had known for years could have deliberately attacked her own daughter, the child might have been spared a further injury. As it was, the paediatrician at the second hospital kept the girl in hospital under various pretexts while the mother continued psychiatric treatment, until eventually it was felt safe for the girl to return home.

It is often surprising the extent to which experienced doctors can delude themselves on this subject. I recently went to a meeting in a county hospital attended by doctors, police and social workers, which was held in order to discuss the problem of battering. Visiting lecturers from other counties who had made a special study of this field had already described the whole syndrome of battering, and explained what their own counties were doing about it. To my amazement an obviously intelligent and successful doctor from the audience stood up and after making one or two comments, finished by saying with total authority, 'We have *no* cases of baby-battering here in ——shire.' One of the lecturers, a highly experienced police surgeon, replied patiently, 'Nor had we in ——shire, until we looked for them.'

If it is difficult for doctors to suspect patients whom they have known for some time, it must be even more so for social workers. Many families who batter have already had lengthy contact with the social services for various reasons. Some may have been incapable of organizing their daily life, needing advice on how to cope with the weekly rent and hire purchase commitments; others may have been without a regular income because of the father's unemployment or imprisonment. Perhaps an older child has already had a brush with the law and is under probation. Social workers may meet their clients two or three times a week for several years on end; under such circumstances they become personally attached to them and so involved in their success in one aspect of their life that they may not notice danger signs elsewhere.

Ray Castle (the present head of the NSPCC Battered Child Research Department) and Angela Skinner wrote in their 1969 *Retrospective Study* :

The need for very skilled social work with these families was apparent. . . There was considerable evidence to suggest agency pressure, together with the emotive nature of the problem, created anxiety in the workers which restricted their ability to offer help. *Many social workers found difficulty in accepting that child battering is a reality.* In the following example the social worker encouraged the parents to find an acceptable explanation for their child's injuries, and the interview was thus worker focused, instead of client focused. 'I pressed with all the questions I could think of, I even suggested the dog, but she assured me she had no idea how the child received the injuries.' In the second interview the worker read to the father the statement that the mother had made. He said it was correct, and strongly maintained that if there had been an accident he would have said so. 'I again suggested all kinds of accidents, but he would have none. I felt he was on the verge of tears.' [my italics]

The authors continue : 'There was some evidence of premature case closing. It appeared that this could have been a result of the worker's anxiety and inability to focus on underlying stress.' In other words, the worker simply could not bring herself to examine the reality of the case, which would have meant facing her own reactions to what her client had done. By pretending not only to them but also to herself that the injury had been purely accidental, she was able to stay on friendly terms with her clients. Raymond Castle has also suggested that some workers may close their cases prematurely because the prospect of the demands which would be made upon them if they were to become fully supporting is too alarming.

Why is it that so many people are unable to accept the possibility that comparatively ordinary people might batter their own children? The most common suggestion put forward is that they cannot face up to the violence within themselves. We have all been taught that violence is bad unless it is officially licensed, as in war. Permitted forms of violence retain their popularity – some people are still calling for the return of flogging and capital punishment. Since we are forced from early infancy to restrain our own violence to the point where we may no longer accept that we possess any aggressive instincts at all, we may be particularly hard on those who carry out unpermitted violent acts. For once you recognize that ordinary people, people not very unlike yourselves, can in certain uninhibited moments do terrible things to their own children, then you have no choice but to accept the possibility that a similar violence might lie within you too. It may be that doctors are particularly prone to this blindness as they have devoted their lives to healing: it may not be possible for some of them to accept that they themselves might also have strong destructive impulses. Certainly it seems strange that, even now, there are many examples of doctors not spotting cases which ought to have been obvious to them.

Even people, such as lawyers, who are professionally involved with crime may find emotional reactions clouding their normally cool judgment when they study the details of the severe injuring of a child. Carolyn Okell writes (*Law Society's Gazette*, September 1969): 'Social workers and doctors, for example, may be so affected by the emotive nature of the subject that their ability to offer therapeutic help is diminished, and lawyers may find excuses for refusing Instructions in these cases.' She quotes the case of a four-month-old infant with 'black eye, bruising on buttocks, bilateral fractured ribs, four long bone fractures, fracture of skull, incomplete amputation of right great toe and laceration of left ear with partial loss of lobe' in order to illustrate the kind of case a lawyer might be asked to handle. She then continues: 'Solicitors practising in the criminal courts sometimes give their clients the impression of being callous. Even the most hardened practitioner, however, must shudder at the list set out above.'

When studying the causes of baby battering it is easy to lull oneself into a sort of woolly-minded kindness; easy, as one imagines oneself in their place, to feel sorry for stressed parents who have given way to their impulses. But every so often one comes across the kind of case quoted above and instantly one's whole attitude changes. Everyone dealing with such families feels this revulsion – nurses, doctors, policemen, social workers – but fortunately extreme cases are becoming rarer as more knowledge is gained. The NSPCC have found that although more cases of battering are being referred to them, the main increase lies with the number of moderately injured children : the proportion of these to seriously injured children has grown considerably. The assumption is therefore that parents under stress are beginning to be picked up early enough to prevent the worst kind of 'accidents' from happening.

How much knowledge do we have of the parents themselves? Who are these people? What has made them act as they do? The answer seems to be that you cannot pinpoint one particular type of personality, but they all have a good deal in common.

First it must be borne in mind that those parents who torture and kill are at the far end of a continuum : at the opposite end are those who have never actually physically battered their children at all. I am thinking here of the kind of mother who sits weeping as she looks hopelessly at the child she feels inadequate to cope with, or of the ineffective father who secretly believes himself a failure in everything he has ever done. Parents like this give their children no enthusiasm for life, no belief in themselves. Often marrying people like themselves they spend their days in a more or less permanent state of depression, ill-organized and only just coping with the demands life makes on them. If they are lucky and their circumstances do not deteriorate, they will probably do no worse than raise vaguely unhappy, uncertain children much like themselves. It is, however, from such a background that many batterers come. This does not mean that all battering backgrounds are necessarily depressive, but almost invariably, however apparently successful and confident the family seems, for one reason or another the abusing parent suffers from a severe lack of self-esteem. It is as though he has one skin less when you compare him with a more integrated personality : he lacks the resilience which self-confidence brings.

Why is this so? What has caused battering parents, so disparate in upbringing, class and intelligence, to be so alike in this one vital aspect? The answer offered by most people studying the problem is that first and foremost a battering parent has been deprived of the one thing almost universally acknowledged to be the necessary foundation for the formation of a fully mature and balanced personality – a satisfactory 'mothering' experience in his infancy. No one suggests that a lack of good mothering is the sole cause for the eventual breakdown of a parent's care of his child, but there are few who would not place it at the top of the list of the handicaps under which battering parents labour.

'Mothering' may be carried out by either a mother or a father or by a substitute parent. It means far more than merely being looked after by a natural mother. Irene Josselyn has summed up motherliness as being the ability to show tenderness, gentleness, and empathy, and to value a love object more than oneself. Joan Court writes, 'It seems that battering parents have not experienced an empathetic, caring relationship with a mother or mothering figure and go through life constantly yearning for such a relationship in spite of their disbelief in the possibility of ever finding it.' She continues that, as a result of never finding the loving reassurances they are still searching for, this 'burden of unmet dependency needs often results in a chronic low-grade depression. The parents complain of loneliness and are usually very socially isolated. Frequently they are apathetic and disorganized in their social functioning, although the latter may not be apparent initially.'

Steele and Pollock, looking at the personality of battering parents from a psychiatric point of view, found that they could not place the parents in their study into any single one of their usual categories. 'On the contrary, they present the wide spread of emotional disorders seen in any clinic population – hysteria, hysterical psychosis, obsessive-compulsive neurosis,

anxiety states, depression, schizoid personality traits, schizo-
phrenia, character neurosis, and so on. . .' However, the one
common trait they did find was that

all of our parents were deprived as infants and children. We are not
concerned here with material deprivation. Some were raised in
poverty with great material deprivation, others in average circumstances, and a few in the midst of material abundance and wealth.
We are referring to deprivation of basic mothering – a lack of the
deep sense of being cared for and cared about from the beginning of
one's life . . . we do not imply that our patients have lacked maternal attention . . . their mothers have hovered over them, involving
themselves in all areas of the patient's life throughout the years.
But . . . this has been in a pattern of demand, criticism, and disregard, designed to suit the mother and leave the patient out.

Thus the mother is trying to produce a child whose excellence will shower credit on her; the actual needs of the child's
own personality are ignored. The child, recognizing quite clearly
that her mother is uninterested in her as she really is, gains no
confidence in her own natural abilities : instead she spends all
her energy trying to please her mother by attempting to become
the kind of person she imagines is wanted. This desire to placate
those in authority may later prevent her from obtaining the
help she really needs; and she cannot help showing only her
best side when she visits people in authority whom she sees as
potential accusers. Often she will manage to convince her
doctor that she is a conscientious person capable of looking
after her child successfully, thus denying herself the very help
she went to him for in the first place. The distraught person
underneath will be completely camouflaged : only the immediate family is allowed to see both sides of her face.

Some will object that almost every human fault nowadays is
blamed on inadequate mothering. Yet battering parents are
caring parents : they desperately want to have a happy home
with happy children. Of all the problem families social workers
have to deal with, these are the ones who are most clearly
motivated to improve themselves. I am not suggesting they are
the easiest to deal with, but there is more hope of helping them

successfully than there is, say, of trying to persuade a not very bright lad fresh out of Borstal to become an honest sober citizen when up to now he has spent his life in a low intelligence family with a long tradition of criminal activities.

It is not therefore a question of *blaming* parents because they are failing to be one hundred per cent perfect, but of looking squarely at whatever facts have already been discovered and saying, this is what we know, and this is where we must begin to tackle the problem. Today's parents are in the process of moulding the next generation, and if these future parents are to be prevented from passing on the disease in their turn, we must stop allocating blame and wade in immediately with every scrap of assistance the State can be persuaded or bullied into providing.

Let us look at one or two illustrations of the memories battering parents have of their home and their parents. Mrs Jones said: 'I'd never had a good relationship with my own mother, I never remember kissing her : we weren't that sort of a family. Even when I got married I didn't kiss her or anything like that'; and later, 'My father always worshipped boys, and my brothers always had preference at home . . . they've got several photos on the sideboard of my two brothers, but there aren't any of me and my sisters, not one. My eldest sister, I think *she* could have been classed as a battered child, though you didn't have them then, did you?'

Steele and Pollock believe battering parents have ambivalent feelings about the mother image, seeing it as potentially good and bad, with emphasis on the bad side. They reported a dream of one of their patients, Penny. 'I was with mother. There was the usual feeling of tension. It was like we were in a motel and we had gone to bed in twin beds. I woke up. Something in white was standing over me very threatening. It was terrifying. I called to my mother for help. She answered, "I am your mother," and it turned out that she, herself, was the creature in white who was threatening me. I woke up screaming!' Steele and Pollock go on to explain that battering parents typically feel that the people they turn to for help are untrustworthy and may attack instead of helping. This patient had bad problems with her punitive feelings towards her five-month-old son, and she feared she was no better a parent than her own mother had been, and that no help would ever be forthcoming.

They also comment that although motherliness may seem oriented towards women, it applies equally to men.

In our view there is no essential difference in the origin of motherliness in men and women. In both sexes it involves a pre-gender identification in the infant's early life with the mother's behaviour. In males later masculine strivings and identifications may allow persistence of motherliness or diminish it. In females the early motherly identification becomes woven into the normal psycho-sexual development leading to motherhood and identification with the child-bearing woman. Most simply, we believe child-caring and child-bearing behaviours have separate and distinct origins.

As to whether more males or females attack, there is no clear-cut answer: different studies show diametrically opposed results. Everything seems to depend upon where and how the studies are carried out, and who is organizing them. For example, in their *Retrospective Study of Seventy-eight Battered Children* (1969) the NSPCC found that in forty-two cases it was the woman who had battered, in thirty-three cases the man and in three cases the two were in very close collusion. Other reports (mostly American) show as many men as women battering, and a few even showed a predominance of men. But the study carried out by Steele and Pollock found that in fifty instances it was the mother who was the attacker and in only seven cases the father.

An important factor controlling which sex predominantly batters is the financial position of the parents. A middle- or upper-class man in a really good job has several strong incentives to keep on working, whereas an unskilled labourer will expect to be unemployed occasionally. Bearing in mind that battering parents have basic problems of stability and self-esteem which could lead to a higher than normal mobility of employment, fathers in the lower income groups are likely to be around the house more than the businessman arriving home after the children are in bed. The consequent interactions between father and child in the first case will thus be more pronounced.

We have now arrived at another feature which is said to be typical of such families, that they not only change their jobs frequently but they also change their houses, sometimes to the point where they might be labelled nomadic. In 1969 the NSPCC reported problems with accommodation in 35 per cent of the families, though many apparently left their district to escape from the criticism of their neighbours and also from the various social bodies hot on their heels. A later report published by the NSPCC in September 1972 showed similarly high figures of families moving from their homes during and after the time they came to the attention of the NSPCC.

Flight may also mean escape from debts, such as hire purchase commitments, television rentals, or rent arrears, the last a common problem. For many it is also a flight from reality, a belief that a change of environment will bring better times. Frequently immature mentally, the battering parents often cling almost childishly to the hope that everything will be better tomorrow.

The mere fact of being investigated can be enough to make a family leave a district, even when they have not yet battered a child severely enough for the local authorities to be able to place a Care Order on them and arrange for regular supervision. This means, of course, that the children are still at risk but are now in an area where the family is unknown and unsupervised. Since such families rarely leave forwarding addresses, tragedy may be the result if the new situation does not work out as successfully as the parents had hoped.

The NSPCC figures seem to confirm the suggestion that batterers are frequently nomadic, but the bias of the NSPCC's caseload towards the working classes must be borne in mind. Dr A. Jackson, Consultant Paediatrician at the London Hospital in the heart of the East End, finds the nomadic habits of many of his working-class patients difficult to cope with, regardless of what they have come to see him about. Medical records needed to check up on previous vaccinations or details about old illnesses are often impossible to trace because the patient has moved several times over the last few years and no longer remembers his doctor's address, if he was ever officially registered at all. Dr Jackson personally doubts if the restlessness of the battering parents he deals with is much more than a natural part of their social environment. One might add that the breakup of the old working-class structure where several generations lived permanently within reach of each other is no doubt responsible for much of the added stress on younger people today.

We don't know how nomadic middle- and upper-class battering families are : there are no statistics to tell us. However, being less easily mobile, they are very unlikely to shift about as much as poorer families do. Not only is the father's job likely to tie them down to a particular area, they will traditionally own their accommodation either by outright purchase or by a long lease. Removal is therefore a considerably more complicated business than changing one weekly-rented set of rooms for another. Another important factor is that they will have less outside pressure to move from social workers and neighbours. As one mother living in a council tower block who had battered her small daughter, complained, 'You can't imagine what it's like, everyone in the whole block knowing why all these people from the social services keep coming. My regular social worker, she comes twice a week and she has to walk through the estate past the other blocks, then up two flights of stairs and along that long corridor outside. Dozens of my neighbours see her, and they all know she's coming to see me and *why* she's coming to see me. It's horrible. Sometimes I feel like getting right away where nobody knows me.' Not many NSPCC officers or health visitors knock on doors in upper suburbia : private medical treatment is more discreet.

One of the inevitable results of this nomadic life is that many families find themselves without roots in the community in which they are at present living. Talking about the importance of having intimate and long-lasting local ties with the Constabulary of a district where many expatriates from London work in the new factories, I found that the police had no doubt about the effect such uprooting causes. It is not only among these 'foreign' workers, however, that they are finding an increased incidence of problems of all kinds; they also feel sure that in the villages where an older style of life still prevails there is less crime and fewer problems than among those who have moved into the new housing estates. As the woman police sergeant put it, 'when you've got Mum round the corner and Gran up the street you watch out, you can't get away with anything then. But who knows or cares in the new suburbs? They're cut off from everyone there, and they don't know a soul to talk to.'

What with trying to keep up with changes of address, and the reluctance of many of these mothers to keep appointments, social workers have a difficult time of it. Joan Court, warning midwives that it was not much use urging unwilling mothers to come to their clinics, suggested instead that the midwives' energy be spent in establishing a warm and friendly relationship with them. 'Battering parents are usually very lonely and isolated people, often ashamed even of going out of the house; they are afraid of making friends because they expect to be let down, and so may appear distant, elusive and hostile. They seldom have roots in the community and are usually distant from a helpful grandmother, or find their own parents critical and rejecting.'

When we first asked ourselves who battering parents are, we discovered that the one thing which is firmly established is that they have been deprived of good 'mothering', as a result of which they lack self-esteem, frequently to a crippling extent. Additional facts, such as that batterers may be of either sex, that they are often nomadic and therefore without local roots, are important, but time and time again we keep coming back to this severe lack of self-esteem. I shall therefore devote the last part of this chapter to looking at the origins and results of their lack of self-esteem, for it is here that the whole root of the problem seems to lie.

It is difficult for naturally confident people to put themselves in the place of a person who is not only certain that he can never do anything right, but also that no one will ever really like him, and that therefore no one will be willing to help him in times of trouble. A child needs to be convinced from earliest babyhood that he is wanted and is loved, no matter what he does; smiles with no warmth behind them cannot fool him. As with animals, it is the wordless communication which counts. If the certainty that one is wanted and loved is ingrained, most problems can be tackled with a confidence which in itself is often enough to solve many difficulties, especially where dealings with other people are concerned. But the unconfident mother or father, faced with a stressful situation, has no inner certainty to fall back on.

Nevertheless, it might be argued, most unconfident people do not batter their children. Perhaps the most important 'extra' motivating battering parents is that their own parents had unrealistic expectations of them, and now they are making similar demands of their own children. These high expectations can take many forms : each parent will have his own particular needs and ideas of the perfect child. The one demand that all battering parents seem to have in common, however, is that their children should be absolutely obedient. As one twenty-three-year-old father said when he was questioned by the NSPCC after he had 'lost his temper' with his child : 'I love my children and I wouldn't want them to grow up disobedient . . . when I say jump, I want them to jump.' He admitted that he was 'beyond control' himself when he was a child (though this may well have been his parents' view of his behaviour rather than the actual reality) and he was determined that his own baby son should not be the same.

High expectations do not necessarily bring about a lack of self-esteem, of course – many a person has ridden to success through the prodding of ambitious parents – but it must be possible for these expectations to be fulfilled. This is the centre of the problem. The demands these parents make cannot be fulfilled because they are unrealistic. The child is therefore pre-doomed to failure and a growing certainty of his total inability ever to do anything right.

Together with this insistence on absolute obedience usually

goes a pathetic demand for clearly expressed love. The parents want what they never had in their own infancy – uncritical love – and who better than their own children to give it to them? Unfortunately they do not realize that small children are very self-occupied creatures: infants need to pass through many stages of development before they are ready to offer selfless love to anybody. Sadly, some parents do nevertheless manage to wrest some precocious sympathy from their babies at an age when no child should have to face such demands. Small children hardly capable of talking can sometimes be seen running to comfort a clearly distressed parent after a family row: such children often develop an anxious air as they watch to see what is going to be needed of them.

This demand may begin from birth. One nineteen-year-old mother flung down her ten-week-old son causing severe injury to his skull, because he didn't love her. When asked why she thought that, she replied that he wouldn't stop crying no matter what she did for him and that proved he couldn't love her, didn't it? If he had loved her he would have smiled at her instead of crying all the time.

Steele and Pollock came to the conclusion that all the parents they had been studying had been brought up in the manner in which they were now bringing up their own children. The excessive demands made on the parents when they were young, which they were incapable of fulfilling, had made them feel that all they did was

erroneous, inadequate, and ineffectual. No matter what the patient as a child tried to do, it was not enough, it was not right, it was at the wrong time, it bothered the parents, it would disgrace the parents in the eyes of the world, or it failed to enhance the parents' image in society. Inevitably, the growing child felt, with much reason, that he was unloved, that his own needs, desires and capabilities were disregarded, unheard, unfulfilled, and even wrong. *These factors seem to be essential determinants in the early life of the abusing parent; the excessive demand for performance with the criticism of inadequate performance and the disregard of the child as an individual with his own needs and desires.* Everything was oriented toward the parent; the child was less important [my italics].

In addition to these factors, Steele and Pollock feel that suppressed aggression also helps to increase the parents' lack of self-esteem :

at the [same] time the parent is making demands and attacks upon the infant, he is also frustrating some of the infant's most basic needs for comfort and empathy. Such frustrations are repetitive stimulations to the basic aggressive drive. Stimulation of the aggressive drive with its accompanying anger toward the frustrating caretaker [i.e. the mother or father] coupled with the parallel development of strict superego rudiments, inevitably leads to a strong sense of guilt. This guilt, largely unconscious, predominantly in relation to the mother, persists through the patient's life, and leads to turning much of the aggression inward toward the self. *It accounts in the adult for the frequent periods of depression and contributes to the pervasive sense of inferiority and low self-esteem* [my italics].

So, by the age of three or four, the small child has already been moulded into the shape of a future battering parent. His aggressions are well on the way to being fully developed, he has learned that adults are strict people who punish severely if they are not instantly obeyed, who demand love and don't give it, who are never satisfied and always super-critical. As a parent he will still suffer from feelings of guilt, hopelessness, even uselessness, but he will probably not be able to avoid acting as he has been taught adults should act, even though he wants above all to make his children happier than he was when he was young. He will not inevitably batter; he may be fortunate and have a succession of kindly understanding teachers, gaining some confidence from doing well at school, he might even find the right marriage partner and have good luck in his employment – but if none of these things happen, at best his life will be a difficult one; at worst, he might end up attacking his children in the way he had been taught at his mother's knee.

Let us put ourselves in the place of a woman brought up in this manner. All of us who are parents have probably spent some hours in the middle of the night attempting to persuade an unwilling baby to fall asleep. Stressed parents' babies seem to wake more often than others: whether this is because the parents' nervousness is passed on or whether parents are nervous because they do not have enough sleep, who can say? Imagine then that night after night, sometimes several times every single night, you are awoken by a crying baby. It lies there snug and warm in its blankets while you rock it backwards and forwards, backwards and forwards, half-frozen. Can you not feel how eventually such a mother's control might crumble, how she might find irresistible the desire to fling the baby down, to fling it anywhere as long as she can get rid of it? A child psychiatrist talking to me about this kind of situation, said more than half-seriously, 'It's not the fact that some parents bash their babies which surprises me, but the fact that most parents don't!'

At this point it might be asked, if these parents feel so bad about their child and themselves, why don't they get help, tell someone about their troubles? One answer is that from their earliest infancy they have learned that asking is not the same as getting. They are convinced they are not the kind of people whom others think highly enough of to bother about.

Let us look at a very simplified example of how such a pattern might evolve. We start with a baby. A tiny child knows instinctively how to look pathetic: its eyes brim with tears, its lips tremble, and its sadness is so irresistible any mother who happens to be around will long to pick it up and cuddle it. Any mother, that is, except the baby's own mother, who may well be behind in her schedule, exhausted from a crying session in the middle of the night, and possibly already pregnant with another child. Nevertheless most mothers, even in these circumstances, somehow raise up enough energy to manage some kind of warm reaction. Even if they slam out of the room angrily, within a few minutes they are usually back feeling mean, and ready to patch up the quarrel. For a quarrel it is: one thinks of quarrelling as necessarily verbal, but the exchange of emotions between mother and child in such a situation is no less powerful and perceived by both sides simply because one participant cannot speak.

What of the child who tries screaming when its lip-trembling is unsuccessful, but only receives a hard slap for his pains? His lesson is a simple one and quickly taught – he learns that it is no use expecting a comforting answer to his signals for help. In later life, faced with exactly the same situation but reversed, the now grown-up uncomforted child gazes at its own infant, and is momentarily paralysed by a turmoil of emotions. If the child was a female and is now the mother, her guilt is added to by the universal expectation that she will instinctively know *how* to 'mother'. She stands there wanting to do so many different things, only some of which are conscious. She wants to pick up the distressed child and comfort it because she loves it. But she also sees in the crying child herself as an infant and automatically feels guilt because her own mother hated her crying and made it quite clear she did so. In addition she is angry with the child because she had expected it to give her the love she feels she never had when she was young, and now the little brat is bawling its head off at her instead of smiling and showing its love. Obviously it doesn't love her any more than her own mother did. She both sympathizes with the frustration the child must be feeling at being ignored but also feels frustrated herself that yet once more she has failed, has produced an unloving snivelling little thing which must be punished or it will never grow up right.

At this early stage such ambivalence of feelings might result in little more than the mother shouting at the child, or perhaps slapping its hand. Quite likely she will take her baby to her doctor with some trivial excuse, perhaps about a non-existent rash on its arm or her concern that it isn't sitting up yet; she might even complain it doesn't sleep. Unfortunately, because she does not really expect help, and because she learned as a child to appease authority at all costs, she does not come out with the one vital fact which is eating her away – that sometimes she wants to hurt her baby to an extent which terrifies her.

The doctor sees a clean, tidy mother and a clean, tidy baby with nothing physically wrong with it, and decides the mother is one of those irritating women who fuss over every detail, wasting a great deal of his time. Outside waiting in his surgery he has perhaps a woman suffering from breast cancer, a man with angina, a young unmarried girl who wants an abortion, and a couple of new patients – is it any wonder he brushes off the fussing mother with a few words of reassurance that the baby will grow out of whatever it is she has complained about, adding perhaps a prescription for a dose of something or other, intended to shut up the mother rather than the baby?

The mother returns home, perhaps not knowing why she is so unhappy when the doctor has just reassured her that nothing is wrong, or possibly she knows perfectly well why. She is not too badly stressed – her husband, though inadequate in many ways, means well and she is fond of him – but debts are accumulating and she has a suspicion she may be pregnant again already. Two or three days later she smacks the baby much harder than she meant to when it wouldn't stop struggling while she changed its nappy, and she is horrified at the red mark that stays on its skin. Again she goes to the doctor with some excuse, and again he dismisses her, this time rather more brusquely. Perhaps she makes two or three more of these 'cries for help' as they are called, but she is unlucky : either her doctor hasn't studied the subject of battered babies or he thinks it's all exaggerated – what such parents need is self-control. Either way he doesn't connect it with this particular mother.

The day her baby is six months old the sun is shining and she suddenly feels unaccountably happy. She spends most of the morning preparing a special lunch for the baby to celebrate its first half year. Unfortunately the baby doesn't like changes in its diet and spits it out. The mother's mood switches disastrously : once more she is rejected, her efforts are despised and flung back at her unwanted. She snatches the baby out of its high-chair and throws it on the floor.

When, next day, she takes it to her doctor's surgery and explains away the cut on its forehead and the surrounding bruising by saying it fell out of its cot, he accepts the explanation. The next time she loses her temper she takes the baby to the outpatients' clinic at a hospital several miles away : this time it has a heavy bruise round its mouth where she thrust the bottle at it so hard it cut the skin of the lips. Again she is unlucky : it has been a bad day and the casualty officer is exhausted because he was up half the night deputizing for a colleague ill with 'flu. He knows a little about battered babies : he went to a lecture on them a couple of years ago when he was a student. He sees the nearly healed scar on this one's forehead and, as he examines the cut lip and bruised mouth, at the back of his mind a warning bell is ringing. But the mother is so obviously concerned, a pleasant anxious woman, half in tears about her baby; there are a dozen people queueing to see him; he is so sleepy himself he can hardly keep his eyes open and anyway, it is only theory he has learned – he has never actually met a case of battering but surely this isn't the kind of woman who would... He tells the nurse to apply a plaster.

The next time might have been the last time. The mother, now over three months pregnant, has flung her baby so hard against the wall she has fractured its skull. This time she runs to the local hospital with it, doesn't wait, because she knows it is serious. Here the casualty officer is more alert, he calls the sister, a very experienced woman, who instantly senses the situation. The baby is X-rayed, taken into hospital, and the mother is seen by the paediatrician who, fortunately, is sympathetic. No charges are preferred, and after several months the baby is allowed home to the mother who is now under supervision from a very helpful social worker. She will need help for a long time to come, but the baby is safe now; the family has been lucky.

This is only a simplified imaginary case, but the pattern of injury and cries for help is typical. So many children are injured at first in places that can be easily seen – small cigarette burns on the hand, bruising on the face, especially around the mouth – that we must assume that the parents are placing a kind of stigmata on the child as an overt cry for help. Sadistic parents cover up their crimes; what is done, is done in secret. Battering parents nearly always start by hitting where it shows, and then taking the child to a doctor. Often when a coroner makes investigations about a dead child he finds it has been taken at various times to several hospitals, but since there is no liaison between hospitals no one is conscious of the steady progression of the severity of the battering, except the parent responsible.

The pity is that most of these parents cannot bring themselves to communicate their distress overtly because it means admitting their failure once again. Their self-esteem is so low they *cannot* reveal themselves. Those such as Mrs Jones are lucky : she was able to communicate, to say what was wrong, so she could be helped before it was too late.

Carolyn Okell reported an American social worker as saying : 'It soon becomes evident that this sort of person is a very self-defeating person. Therefore, if the patient defeats you in the process of defeating himself, remember he has had lots of practice doing himself in.' Ray Castle, referring to the fact that often these parents will not admit their feelings even to themselves, writes : 'The fact that the child battering adult was often unaware of the basis of the problem and unable to be explicit, was one reason why it received so little attention from social workers. A clean and tidy home and outward concern for the child's welfare often obscured the problem.'

So there these parents are, locked up in themselves, unable to ask for help, torn between love and hate for the child, and pity and hate for themselves. As we shall see in a later chaper, they rarely receive much support from their marriage partners as they tend to choose people much like themselves. Often, it is very difficult to disentangle who has actually done the battering, and sometimes the truth is never discovered.

This sad little story illustrates several of the points we have been talking about, particularly the excessive demand for excellence which is the background to many battering parents' own childhood. A middle-class mother who had attacked her child talked about her own infancy. 'My mother would have made a marvellous foster mother to small babies. She wanted a perpetual baby. She loved me when I was small and helpless, but she rejected me from the day I first said "No"... Ever after that she told me I was wicked... I could never please her – I can still see myself running home from school and not daring to tell her I had a sum wrong. I had to have ten out of ten and not just that, I'd have to be the only one in the class with ten out of ten. I desperately longed for her approval, but I was never in a state of grace. She always looked reproachful and angry and said if I was so naughty she would have to go to prison. I think I grew up to believe all babies were bad once they got to a year or so old.'

Who was to blame? Certainly not the baby son, who was clearly blameless. The mother? But perhaps she could not do otherwise, given her own childhood and her present circumstances. The grandmother? But what had happened to *her* to make her so heartless to her own child, when clearly she loved small babies? How was it she had become so mutilated and so destructive? Researchers are now finding the likelihood of a long chain of many generations' growth. It is true that the members of each new generation have a fresh opportunity to break their own links, but they start heavily handicapped in comparison to most of us. Had Mrs Jones's husband, for example, not developed the illness which finally sent him blind, Mrs Jones might have succeeded in overcoming her difficulties. Although she insisted that her family life was very happy before her husband's illness ('ideally happy', she once said), she also admitted she had been rather harsh on her older son and had expected a great deal of him. Nevertheless, she had tried hard to be fair to both her son and her daughter in spite of her prejudice against boys, and would probably have made a better job of bringing up her children than had her own parents. But when the stress became too severe – her husband turned impotent, his subsequent change of character, the unexpected shortage of money, the incessant quarrels, the taking of a lover only to lose him – her reserves of strength were inadequate. The lover's child, unfortunate in being a boy, became the scapegoat for all her anguish.

Sometimes I have heard the comment that this is a terrible century which allows such things to happen. But is not the opposite the truth? The fact is that we are the first century to take it for granted that such things should *not* be allowed to happen. From the beginning of history children have suffered their share of man's brutality to man. Many early societies – Babylonian, Egyptian, Greek, Roman – did not even consider newly-born children as full members of the human race until they had been purified by special rites, unwanted children being exposed or disposed of in other ways. Infanticide has always been a common way of solving the embarrassing problem of illegitimate babies or of babies born to overcrowded families in times of war, famine or deep poverty. As for child abuse, from the early Egyptians onwards to the present day, children have been whipped, beaten and humiliated in order to help them learn, most parents encouraging teachers to be ruthless in the treatment of their charges.

Purposeless cruelty to children has also always existed : old records report children being deliberately burned, stuck with pins, left unclad in winter, starved, beaten and kicked, and only when treatment became so gross that neighbours could no longer ignore it was action taken. The appalling system of baby-farming which reached its height in the last century was responsible for the slow death, usually by starvation or poisoning, of many thousands of babies. The ruling classes, many of whom knew quite well what was happening, made no attempt to have the practice stopped, possibly because they themselves were partly responsible for the system by their purchase of wet-nurses, who were thereby forced to farm out their own babies.

Setting small children to work was another cruelty which frequently inflicted worse torture than most baby batterers commit today. Large-scale industrialization resulted in many children of six or seven years old working in the mills from 6 a.m. to 7 or 8 in the evening. If they fell asleep at their job they would be whipped or pinched awake, or cold water thrown over them. In the mines half-clad girls of nine or ten dragged truckloads of coal from the face to the foot of the shaft, crawling on all fours in the narrow seams, their hands and knees streaming with blood and encrusted with dirt, at the mercy of the half-brutalized miners. Many of these young workers did not live to grow up, some dying of disease, overwork and malnutrition, others of suicide.

Perhaps the worst-treated children of all were the young chimney-sweeps who were forced to crawl about inside still-hot chimneys, half-suffocating from the stench and loose soot. Sold for a few guineas to their masters, many of these boys died of cancer of the scrotum and of consumption, and the health of most was ruined, but almost up to the end of the last century the public continued to ignore legislation intended to stamp out the practice because alternative methods of cleaning old-fashioned chimneys were less effective. It was not only at work that last century's children suffered, however: Victorian fathers of all social classes frequently chastised their children so severely and expected such perfection of manners and behaviour from them that much of their treatment would today be classified as battering. Yet in their epoch they were seen as admirable men.

If it is borne in mind that child abuse has been a continuing factor in nearly all societies throughout history, the cases outlined in the following chapter may then be seen in their proper historical perspective. Today we look at the world with very different eyes from those of our ancestors, but man cannot change his nature overnight, and it is pointless to expect him to do so.

Chapter 3

The violent end of the spectrum

Consider the following items – mostly recent newspaper reports, one a doctor's report – on parents who have either killed their children or caused them permanent physical or emotional damage. Death itself seems to come arbitrarily: whether it is a particular slap, a particular punishment which kills, or whether the child suffers years of ill treatment before his body finally succumbs, frequently seems to depend on chance. The pattern of increasingly severe attack is there, and its eventual end depends on whether successful intervention comes in time.

In this first case the father is being sued for divorce by his wife; the death of the younger child happened several years before this suit was brought: 'A father who illtreats his infant child is being cruel to the mother, Mr Justice Faulks said in the Divorce Court yesterday. "It goes without saying," he commented when giving judgement in a case in which a mother accused her husband of injuring their two children. The younger, aged two months, died.

'The judge said, "I am satisfied that the child got her injuries as a result of violence by her father who suffers unfortunately from an uncontrollable temper." She had four broken ribs, bruises, and a minor break in an arm, which had happened fourteen days earlier. The judge granted a decree nisi to the wife ... because of cruelty by her husband... He denied cruelty. Speaking of the injuries to the daughter, Mr Justice Faulks said that when the eldest suffered a bruise on her right eye and temple the husband said she had fallen against a chair. The wife was in hospital at the time.'

Earlier '... the elder girl broke her leg. The husband said he had found her lying on the floor by her cot. The judge found that great violence by the husband had fractured the girl's leg. The younger child died in June 1967, the judge went on. "The mother heard a noise like a thump, sounding like a car door closing. She found her husband in the sitting room, holding the baby, bouncing her up and down on his knee with a good deal more force than she thought was right. The mother remonstrated when he banged the baby's back. She would have remonstrated more had she known at that time the baby had four broken ribs," the judge went on.

'At the time of the marriage in 1964, the judge said, the husband was described as a gymnastic instructor. "He has the unusual ability of being able to break a substantial log of wood on his head by what he calls karate, or the exercise of mind over matter."

'The husband's counsel had agreed that both children exhibited the "battered baby syndrome". The only question was who was responsible, father, mother or both.' (*The Times*)

The next case describes a household which had a bizarre and quite horrifying method of junishment. 'A father found a cruel and drastic way of punishing his three-year-old son for crying. He grabbed hold of the boy and put him in a hot oven. The boy, Anthony H—, screamed with pain, and was pulled out of the oven by his mother. But, by then, he had been badly burned. Words printed on the bottom of the oven were imprinted on his skin. And the scars left on his body after the ordeal are likely to stay for life, a judge heard at Nottingham Assizes yesterday.

'Anthony's father, H—, admitted causing grievous bodily harm to his son. Mr John Coward, prosecuting, said that H—, a twenty-nine-year-old miner, had three children. When he returned home on 5 February after working a night shift they were making a noise. "He told them to stop but they carried on," Mr Coward said.

'It was then that H— put Anthony in the oven, next to a fire which had been on all day. Mr Coward said that H— left the room. His wife, Gwendoline, pulled Anthony from the oven.

'The couple tried to cover up the burns with bandages, but the boy's injuries were seen by neighbours who told the police. Detective Sergeant Frank Barker said that Anthony later spent eleven days in hospital.

'In a statement H— said, "We always tell the children we will put them in the oven if they don't stop crying. Anthony wouldn't stop so I put him in."

'. . . Mr Justice Caulfield said that the case was one of "shocking cruelty". He said he appreciated that H— had been working hard and wanted to sleep. "But all parents face irritation from their children," the judge added. H— was jailed for three years.' (*Daily Mirror*)

The next two events happened within a few weeks of each other. 'A young man who fractured the skull of a twelve-month-old baby girl when he slapped her was gaoled for three years at Leeds Assizes yesterday. B—, a fitter . . . , who slapped the child to stop her screaming, admitted a charge of manslaughter. Mr Donald Herrod, prosecuting, said that the baby was found dead in her cot about four days later. "For a period of about four days she had been in a semi-conscious state with her young life slipping away and no one thought fit to call a doctor," he said.' (*The Times*)

'W— S—, aged 50, unemployed . . . , was charged at Poole Magistrates' Court yesterday with causing his son, aged 18 months, grievous bodily harm by rubbing his chest and back with sandpaper. He was remanded in custody for a week.' (*The Times*)

As there is a growing understanding of the nature of battering, many parents found guilty are being treated more leniently. 'A man who broke bones in all his baby son's limbs and caused serious brain injury to the child was put on probation for two years yesterday. The baby, three weeks old at the time of injury, was still blind. Norwich Crown Court was told:

'His trouble was that he tried too hard – he tried to be mother as well as father,' said his counsel, Sir Harold Cassel, Q.C.

'Putting P— N— on probation, Mr Justice May told him: "I propose taking a surprising course with you. I think that you have been punished, and will be punished quite sufficiently, for the rest of your life." '

Behind these brief newspaper reports lie months of professional investigation into the lives of the families concerned, the results of which give judges a basis on which to found their decisions. How these various professional bodies – paediatricians, police, social workers, etc. – interact with each other will be looked at in following chapters. For the moment we are concerned with what may be the first report to be written on a particular family, the doctor's report when the injured child is first carried into hospital. Here is a carefully presented report on a fourteen-month-old baby girl who died the day after being brought into hospital, written by the examining doctor who happened to be particularly interested in the problem of battered babies. A few details have been changed to prevent recognition, and some of the medical matter has been shortened, otherwise it is exactly as written.

Medical report on Susan Heston

'I was called to the Emergency and Accident department of this hospital at 9.30 p.m. on 4 July 19— to examine the above-named child who had been admitted at 6.45 p.m. following an accident at home. On examination she was obviously extremely ill and was receiving resuscitation treatment from members of the surgical staff of the hospital for what appeared to be a major intra-abdominal lesion.

She was clean and well nourished.

The following cutaneous marks were present:

FACE

1   a ½″ diameter bruise on the right side of the forehead midway between the eyebrow and the hairline.

2   a ¼″ diameter bruise just above the centre of the left eyebrow.

3   a slightly smaller bruise about 1″ above and slightly to the left of the previous bruise.

[Three other similar bruises to the face are then described.]

BACK A group of three ½″ diameter bruises, with triangular spacing, was present immediately to the left of the spine of the 12th dorsal vertebrae. [Similar details are then given for various marks on the chest, the left forearm, the buttocks, and three other isolated bruises are also described.]

X-RAY EXAMINATION X-ray examination of the skull and chest did not reveal any bony or soft tissue abnormality.

PHOTOGRAPHY I took colour transparencies of the marks on the child's skin before she was transferred to the Operating Theatre.

I was informed by Dr L— that the father had told him the child had slipped through his hands whilst he was playing with her by throwing her in the air. She had fallen on the floor and had not been well since the incident. I could not accept that the injuries present were compatible with this history and in view of this I interviewed both parents. Later I was present at an operation carried out on the child by Mr P—, a Consultant Surgeon at this hospital. The small intestine had been ruptured at the junction of the duodenum and jejunum and he was carrying out a repair of the damaged area.'

'The mother, Mrs Heston, aged 22 years told me that at 4.55 p.m. that afternoon she had left the house to buy some food for the baby's supper. She left the child in the care of her father. When she returned at 5.15 p.m. the child, Susan, was sitting on the floor playing with a toy boat. The child was pale. Her husband picked her up and began playing with her, but the child seemed to be strange.

'The mother asked him, "What's to do?" Her husband told her that he had been throwing her up into the air and she had slipped through his hands when he was trying to catch her. She had landed on the floor and he suspected the child had injured her head. The mother thought the child had a lump at the back of the head and seemed lifeless and cried. In view of all this she took Susan to her general practitioner, Dr —, who advised that she should be brought to this hospital.

'She told me there were two other children, and that she had been pregnant at the time of her marriage. Her parents had been against the marriage on religious grounds. She told me that neither of the other children had suffered in any way, and she had never noticed any bruises on their bodies.

'She stated that Susan had always been fit in the past, but that lately she had been somewhat sickly. From time to time she had been sick after meals, and for about four weeks she had noticed bruises around her privates. These frightened her. They appeared and then resolved. However, she never took the child to the doctor because of them. She had also noticed that the child had sometimes developed bruises on the right side of the face if she had gone out and left the child in the care of the father. She stated, entirely spontaneously, that she had become extremely worried about these various marks, and was beginning to wonder whether the father could be responsible for them as they always seemed to occur when she was not around.

'She had noticed that since Susan was dropped by her father when she was four months old the child cried whenever the father picked her up. That incident had resulted in extensive bruising of the child's face.

'She stated they live in a council house, her husband is a bricklayer and financially she is not under any strain. They have been married for four years. The home is not happy : there have been many arguments and she had left him on three occasions. Each time she returned after absences varying between six days and eight weeks. He has assaulted her on several occasions. Once he broke her nose, and she has sustained three or four black eyes; another time she was unable to walk for a week resulting from a kick on her knee, and she has also sustained bruising of the arms. Although she sleeps badly, her husband sleeps well, and they are not disturbed at night by Susan.

'She told me that her husband was in some trouble when he was fourteen for breaking into a youth club with some other boys and causing damage, but he has never been in trouble with the police for violence, although his mother is frightened of his temper. She thinks his father used to hit him a lot when he was a child, and that his childhood was not a happy one.'

'After I had interviewed the mother I saw the father, Thomas Heston, aged 24 years.

'Before beginning to talk he said that it was "one story against another". He told me that while his wife was out shopping he was "chucking" the child up and he missed her on the way down. She landed on her buttocks, fell back and hit her head against the hard floor. She seemed all right at first but when his wife came the child looked pale so they took her to their doctor.

'He says that he has sometimes noticed bruising on Susan's privates. He was vague as to how often, but he had wondered whether this could be due to bouncing her up and down on his knee. He admitted that at first he could not take to Susan. He had hoped they would have a boy as the other two children were both girls. He says he did not bother much about the other two until they were walking, and said that kiddies did not appeal to him.

'He commented that he knew things looked a bit black but he would not hurt the child. He had not noticed any bruises on her face, "that's a certainty".

'When I asked him exactly how he played with her he said he threw her up "as she comes", and she might have been either facing or turned away from him. That night he had thrown her up about eight times.

'He says his marriage is a bit stormy, and feels that his wife thinks more of her home than of him, and he gets a bit jealous. He considers his mother-in-law is a nuisance and he would not trust her. He comes from a large family with four brothers and one sister : they have had their "ups and downs" but generally he gets on not too badly with his parents.

'He says Susan cries when he goes into the room and that this has happened since he dropped her, but she will play with him. He resents this crying.

'I pointed out that I was under certain difficulty in relating the injuries the child sustained to the history that had been given. He was unable to help me in any way. He denied hurting the child or squeezing her face or back and he commented that "it is difficult to get people to believe it is an accident when things look black". He could not understand how the child had hurt her stomach. He was definite that the child had slipped through his hands and landed on her back on the floor. He says that he has hit her in the past when necessary but this has always been on her bottom. He admits he has a quick temper, but says he has never squeezed the child.

'The father's manner during my interview did not impress me. He did not appear to be open, did not look straight at me and gave me the impression that he was worried about being questioned. In comparison the mother's manner was very open, and she appeared to be very anxious to talk about her worries. She admitted that she wished there was "just her and the children". She wishes she had listened to her parents before getting married.

'I was unable to relate the medical findings on this child to the history given by the father. The distribution of the bruises is compatible with having been caused by a squeeze. They are all of the same age and appear to be a day or two older than the abdominal injury. The lack of swelling around them, in my experience, suggests that they were not caused by an impact with a hard object.

'I was concerned about the group of bruises at the level of the 12th dorsal vertebrae. In my experience bruises in this area are very frequently associated with non-accidental head or chest injuries in children. They were of approximately similar age to the bruises on the child's face and I would have great difficulty in accepting that a child had fallen against an object on three separate occasions and injured practically the same spot on her back. These marks could not have been caused by a fall on a flat floor.

'The bruise on the left costal margin could have been inflicted at the same time as the bruises on the back by excessive pressure being applied around the child's waist. The bruises on the back would be caused by the thumb, and the bruise at the front by one of the fingers of the left hand. There were no marks on the child's skull which were compatible with the history that she had fallen backwards banging the back of her head.

'In my opinion the absence of any history of the child's abdomen coming into contact with a hard object whilst being thrown in the air or landing on the floor, means that the abdominal injury must be attributed to a blow from a fist.

'The injury sustained was extremely grave and would obviously carry a high risk of danger to the child's life. The bruises and other skin marks were relatively trivial in nature but in my view indicated that the child had been subjected to minor, deliberate physical ill-treatment over a period of a few days prior to her admission. If the mother's story is accepted then there is a strong probability that ill-treatment of the child has been carried out intermittently since the child was four months old.

'In view of my concern I contacted Inspector Jones of the NSPCC who proposed to investigate the situation further at the child's home the following day.'

'At 10.00 hours on 5 July 19— I re-examined Susan whilst in the ward. She was seriously ill and I was unable to do more than examine her face. I confirmed the presence of the bruises on the right side of the forehead, over the left eyebrow and over the left angle of the mandible. The marks on the left cheek were still present; it was difficult to identify any causative factor but they may well have been caused by finger nails, though with one exception the top layer of the skin was not damaged.

'At 14.00 hours the same day I was informed that the child had died at 13.45 hours. In view of the discrepancies between the injuries that were present and the history that had been given, I informed Detective Chief Inspector L— of the —— Constabulary about the matter.

'At 11.00 hours on 6 July 19— a full skeletal survey of the body of Susan Heston was carried out, but no skeletal damage either recent or old could be demonstrated. At 15.00 hours the same day I attended a postmortem examination carried out by Dr J— on the body of Susan Heston.

'Signed————————'

Mr and Mrs Heston had probably expected immediate accusation and judgement, instead of which a succession of quietly efficient people bustled around them, whisking off their daughter for treatment, taking down details and all the time noting relevant facts such as that they sat apart from each other in the waiting room, and that the wife refused to speak to her husband and would not let him touch her.

Sometimes very little information can be gathered at a first meeting, however sympathetic the interviewer. Often a blank incomprehension of how the baby came to be injured is expressed : A young mother said, 'I thought it was me little girl who did it, with bottle like, it was only thing I could think of. It couldn't have been the toys because she didn't have any. It must have been done Monday 'cos it come out Monday about 11 o'clock, y'know, the bruises like. I thought it was dirt at first, y'know. Then about 2 o'clock me Dad come in and said what's them bruises then, an' I looked properly then. He noticed them right away, y'know. I said they've only just come on this dinner time. Then I think how could she've done it, you know, she'd not been anywhere. Because I only brought her out at 9 o'clock then I put her back to bed 'cos she was tired. The bruises they all come up at once, like, it must've been banged all at the same time, y'know, but it was the one right by the eye worried me, it's a big bump. I could see it wasn't dirt after a bit, you know, when me Dad said that.' The tone was earnest, obviously sincere and worried. If the doctor had not listened to many other such mothers he might have been taken in, might have accepted the mother's denial as the whole truth instead of what it was, a pathetic refusal to admit perhaps even to herself that she, its own mother, had beaten the baby round its head with its milk bottle when she lost her temper that morning, fracturing its skull.

Sometimes it is quite clear who has done the battering. A woman cringes away from a husband who has beaten her as often as he has beaten the children, and is only too ready to tell the doctor what has happened. At other times each partner defends the other, swears all is happiness and gentleness in the family : the bruises, the broken bones, the burn scars have come unexplained out of the air. Where the interviewing doctor has knowledge and time he will be patient, will prise remarks from the parents which they did not mean to give. Sometimes to their surprise they find relief in talking, and perhaps with sufficient skill and luck the truth comes out. But occasionally the real truth is never discovered; it is only known that this child will never be able to see, and that one will need operations year after year because the growth of one side has been affected : continuous surgery will try to make him more or less symmetrical, but he will always be a little on the short side. In the face of continuous denial by the parents and lack of other evidence, all that can be done is to keep a very close watch on any remaining children and to move in at the first sign of trouble.

A child's life is easily destroyed. Little Emma Brown, pretty, delicate-featured with short blonde hair, came nearer to losing hers than she will ever know. She is lucky : her story has a happy ending. Mrs Brown has been successfully helped and the two of them are reunited. The mother wants to have another baby but acknowledges she will need help. Everyone dealing with her has confidence that she will cope with any new problems as long as she is supported by her new doctor and health visitor, in both of whom she places complete trust. But less than two years ago Emma was brought into hospital with a broken femur and strangulation marks round her neck. She was then four months old. On X-ray previous bone damage was discovered. The interviewing doctor had no doubt in his mind that within a week or two there would have been a further attack which would have killed the child.

Let us listen to his taped interview with the mother who, like Mrs Jones in our first chapter, was prepared to be truthful. Unfortunately for her she could not bring herself to be completely open until it was almost too late; although in her defence it must be said that several professional people knew the state she was in and might have been expected to draw more worrying conclusions from her cries for help than they seem to have done. Only a few details have been altered to prevent identification.

The doctor's voice is quiet, very gentle and friendly, with no suggestion of accusation. The girl is almost breathless with misery, at times hardly able to get her words out. It was only the night before that her baby was brought into the hospital and she has no idea what will happen to her or to it.

'How old are you, now?'

'Twenty-three.'

'And you've been married for how long?'

'Nearly two years.'

'Just one or two more details... What does your husband do for a living?'

'He's a postman.'

'He's around the house a fair bit, then?'

'Not all that much. We've got an allotment, and he spends a lot of his spare time there.' Long pause. 'It helps, you know, the vegetables and that.'

'Are you pushed for money, then?'

'No, we're all right really, because we were lucky with our house. It was my grandma's, you see, and she left it to us, so we're not badly off really.'

'The baby, now. How old is she?'

'Four months old.'

'Right. Now, what did you feel like after baby was born?'

'I felt very happy about everything. The first week in hospital everything was fine. It wasn't till I got home the trouble started. She was a very colicky baby, she had trouble getting her wind up. My husband and I spent hours with her trying to get her off to sleep, but we couldn't, it didn't matter what we did. She just couldn't settle. That's when it all started.'

'Do you know why she had that trouble?'

'No, I think it was the milk she was having, it wasn't the same as the hospital's. I was going frantic reading all the books, wondering what to do.'

'Did you see your doctor?'

'No, but the health visitor came round and she was very good, she sort of helped me along and advised me on things.'

'And that helped?'

'I must admit I was still a bit on edge because the baby was crying all the time and I just couldn't get her to settle. That's what unnerved me, and I got a bit weepy.'

'And what was the first time you ever ... got a bit rough with baby?'

'It must have been when she was about two months old, but I can't remember exactly what I did now. When I came to my mind I was shaking her, but I can't remember properly.'

'So you got hold of her and shook her?'

'Yes.'

'And how was she after that?'

'She was crying a bit afterwards, I must have upset her. I realized what I'd done and I was trying to comfort her, I was trying to love her and make it up to her.'

'Did you tell anyone about this?'

'No, I didn't even tell my husband at first, but I had to in the end, I couldn't keep it to myself any longer.'

'And what was the next time after that?'

'Quite honestly, I don't remember now. At first when it happened I felt so awful about it, but as time got on and I'd do something worse, whatever I'd done in the past didn't seem to matter as much because I was hurting her that little bit more each time and the earlier things seemed trivial in comparison.'

'How many times do you think you hurt her altogether?'

'It's difficult to say. The last three or four weeks maybe just once in every day, but some days not as bad as others.'

'Did you go at all to the doctor about it?'

'Yes. He gave me capsules and tablets but they didn't do an awful lot of good. Then he passed me onto Mr B—, he's a psychiatrist, and he put me on electric treatment for two weeks. But I didn't feel much different. I kept hoping each day I'd feel a bit better, that the effect might come after, but I'm afraid I didn't feel very much different.'

'Did you tell any of the doctors of the rough handling you were giving to Emma?'

'Yes, I told the doctor at the hospital, and I told my own doctor.'

'Did either of them do anything about it?'

'No, not really. They only tried the electric treatment or tablets.'

'Did either of them see the baby?'

'Yes, my own doctor did, not the other one.'

'Now, baby was admitted last night. Can you tell me what happened?'

Long pause. Then: 'I'm afraid I can't throw an awful lot of light on this. I got into such a state yesterday morning...'

'What got you into such a state?'

'I got myself all worked up because she wouldn't settle, and I tried everything for her – I brought up her wind, I changed her nappy, and loved her; I just couldn't get her to settle at all. My husband had gone to work and I got so worked up about it I just didn't know what to do or where to go or who to turn to. I'm afraid I must have shaken her and ... well, I just don't know what else ... I'm afraid I can't remember.'

'You accept the fact that you've broken the limbs...?'

After a long pause she says almost inaudibly, 'It can only be me, I can't see it can be anything else.'

They discuss where she has been brought up, and it emerges that her mother lives some distance away so that a couple of months might go by without them seeing each other. Although her mother is on the telephone she herself cannot afford to have one. She does sometimes talk about her problems with a friendly neighbour, but she doesn't like to inflict her trouble too often on her.

'Do you think it would have helped you if you could have talked to your mother?'

'I think it would have done, just to have someone to talk to. But she wouldn't really understand, she's never gone through it with me and my brother. When I've tried to explain how I feel she tries to understand but I don't think it really sinks in at all.'

'Have you ever thought of trying to tell your health visitor or your doctor about the position between you and your baby?'

'Yes, I spoke to the health visitor more openly than I spoke to my doctor. I spoke quite frankly to her.'

'And she looked at the baby?'

'Yes. And I've taken her to the clinic quite a few times but there was nothing much wrong with her then.'

'Did they know about this problem with. . . ?'

'Yes.'

'Tell me, what was your childhood like?'

Long pause. 'I'm afraid really it wasn't very happy. I didn't really have a very happy childhood. My father and I never really got on, and there was a lot of family trouble. My mother and father didn't really hit it off very well and he was always threatening to emigrate and leave us all. He had this idea if he went to Australia everything would be different. But he didn't want us to go with him and when he was fed up he'd tell us so, say he'd walk out on the lot of us. But when my brother and me started going out with friends, when we got older and I got a boy friend, he got really jealous and was always trying to break it up. There were so many rows I can't tell you. I'm afraid my father and I were never very close, and that's why I wanted it to be so good with the baby. I wanted to be a good mother to her to make up for the past.' She pauses and sighs heavily, then adds in a voice you can only just hear, 'I'm afraid I let myself down though.' After a while she continues : 'My father did try. Any hobby I had he tried to take an interest in, but only because he wanted me to follow in his footsteps. I suppose I didn't take it quite the way he wanted me to, and after a bit when I got different interests he didn't seem to care any more.'

'Can you think of anything anyone might have done which would have helped you before things got to this stage?'

'Well, I don't know. I think if my husband liked going out more it would have helped. When he gets home after doing his rounds he's tired, then after that he goes off to the allotment. He doesn't like going out to the pictures or dancing or anything. He never did and I knew that when I married him. I didn't care much about going out either so it was all right then. But when you've got a baby it's different. I used to go out to work and talk to the other girls, now I'm alone nearly all day and there's no one to talk to and nothing to do in the evening but look at the T.V. I can't talk to John because he's usually worn out by then what with his rounds and digging and that, so he goes to sleep in his chair. I get so bored I just go to bed early, but then I can't always sleep. I'd like to talk to people my own age – maybe I could join a society or something, that might help.'

'What do you feel now that this whole thing's out in the open and you're facing up to it?'

'Well, I realize now what damage I *have* done and I intend to right it, but I'll have to have some sort of help, I realize that. I couldn't do it on my own. All I want now is to make it up to the baby and my husband for what's happened, I want to sort of see things straight.

'I feel very numb at the thought of what has happened to the baby, really, I never thought I could do it. I saw these things in the papers about girls that have hurt their babies, and I used to think how terrible it was and I never thought I could do anything like this. I think I've shocked myself more than anything . . . it seems so terrible.'

'Do you feel relieved in a way now it's out?'

'Well, yes, in a way I do, but at the same time I don't really feel relieved, I feel – like I say – numb. If somebody can help me, if somebody can understand how I feel I'd feel all the better for it. But my doctor, the health visitor, the people at the hospital, my friends, my husband, nobody really understands how I feel about it.'

'What *do* you think we can do to help you?'

'Well, this is it, I don't really know now. I've had the tablets, I've had the electric treatment, I've had one day in hospital and it didn't really do any good. . . I just don't know, I really don't know.'

'How is your husband reacting to all this?'

'He's been very patient and he's very understanding, and he'll try anything to help me, but I think it's been very difficult for him because he's a very different nature to me. He's got far more patience than me and I don't think he sees it quite as he should do. I try explaining to him but he doesn't understand, though he does his best. He'll stand by me. He's been very patient all along. It's not his fault it all happened.'

This interview did not quite end here, but what the mother felt about the help her health visitor had given her, and what the health visitor had to say about the mother's criticisms belongs to the next chapter. Enough has been said, however, to make it clear that had she taken her child to another less alert hospital and not told the truth, and had the injury to its neck not been so obviously suspicious, she might easily have had the baby returned to her with the inevitable result a week or two later.

By now the reader should have a fairly clear picture of various types of battering, and an outline of the various ways the parents are being treated. So much is happening in this field that one doctor commented: 'Every new conference I attend makes what I knew before out of date.' However, he was only talking relatively: there are unlikely to be any dramatic new discoveries. The most important thing that is happening now is that knowledge is spreading even into areas where there has hitherto been a strong reluctance to study the implications of what has been learned about baby battering. The main progress to be made is in the area of cooperation between all the professional bodies concerned. Until there is a drag-net spreading right across the country with a mesh so fine that no parent under stress can slip through it there will continue to be battered babies. Here and there various groups are busy making such a net, and it is from them that the great lessons may be learned.

Chapter 4

Health visitors and social workers

Mrs Brown, who nearly strangled her baby Emma to death, felt that attempts to help her had not been very successful. Her main complaint was that she believed someone had discussed her with her neighbours. When the interviewing doctor asked her what results she had noticed after telling her story to the Health Visitor, she commented: 'Well, I haven't had a great deal of help, really, although they have tried to do their best to help me. I've been very open with the health visitor and I talked a lot to the doctor at the clinic, but the result was that one of them must have spoken to a neighbour and asked her if she would ask me round for a coffee. But that's not the way I wanted it – I can choose my own friends. Obviously this neighbour – and I think a few others as well – know what's going on in my family. It's not very nice when you're not proud of anything you have done: I think it should be kept between the health visitor and the family. I don't like to talk to anyone openly now because I'm frightened of it getting round.'

However, earlier in her conversation with the doctor she told him quite frankly that she had discussed some of her problems with a friendly neighbour – speaking to her as often as every two or three days – so it seems likely she was blaming the health visitor for indiscretions which she perhaps regretted, or possibly had forgotten. Later the interviewing doctor, with the mother's permission, played the tape back to the health visitor and asked her to describe the situation from her point of view.

The health visitor spoke slowly, very thoughtfully, searching always for the truth. 'I think the tape is absolutely accurate. The mother seems to feel we didn't give her a great deal of help, but the real problem is that due to her mental illness it's very difficult to help her.'

'How long have you known her?'

'I visited her first when baby was about eleven days old.'

'What's her condition like now compared to when you first met her?'

'I wouldn't really think it's very different.'

'Do you think she was very depressed after the baby was born?'

'I do. I think she's still depressed.'

'Now, she says that the health visitors didn't give her much help. Did you feel she was responding to your attempts at help at all?'

'She always seemed to be very pleased to see us when we called. In the beginning she was a little suspicious, but when she got to know us she was quite glad to have a visitor. In fact, in the early days we used to go in practically every day to make sure she was having meals and that she was up and about.'

'When she started damaging the baby, what did she tell you about it? Did she say in so many words she was hurting the baby?'

'The only time she gave any indication that she may have damaged the baby was when it was about four weeks old, when she said she threw the baby into the cot. It was examined but there didn't seem to be any evidence of injury to the baby.'

'Who have you discussed this problem with?'

'Well, initially on my first visit to her I decided she was very depressed and mentioned it to her husband, and said that if she got worse she should contact her doctor. Three weeks later she told me she had spoken to her GP who had given her some pills, but she didn't feel they were doing her any good. She said she felt like hitting the baby, so I contacted her doctor and told him that she needed to be seen again urgently, and he arranged to see her. The following week she still didn't seem to be getting any benefit from the treatment, so her own doctor then arranged for her to have an appointment with Dr B—. I then contacted the psychiatric out-patients to check whether an appointment had been made and told them I was worried about the mother's attitude to the baby, as I wanted to make quite sure they realized what the problem was in case she didn't discuss it quite openly with Dr B—.'

'So you notified the possibility of damage to the baby to both her practitioner and the psychiatrist?'

'Yes.'

'Now, she specifically makes the point that she thought someone had been speaking to the neighbours, that you were trying to make friends for her and she wanted to choose her own friends. Would you like to comment on that?'

'This is perfectly true. She was friendly with a girl two doors away, so I asked her if she would see as much of Mrs A— as she could because I felt that she was helping her. We also asked one of the other neighbours if she would include her in one of her coffee mornings. She was new in the neighbourhood, and we felt it would be a good thing for her if the other mothers could include her in their activities.'

'But you didn't tell them anything about the . . . danger to . . .?'

'Oh, certainly not, no!'

'What sort of person would you describe her as?'

'A very . . . withdrawn girl, a very unhappy girl. Not having known her before the mental illness it's difficult to say what sort of personality she has, but she is certainly very inadequate at the moment.'

'Can you think of anything that any of us could have done to have prevented this from becoming a full-scale situation?'

'Well, I feel she should have been admitted with the baby to a place where she could have been kept under constant supervision. It just isn't possible for us to give the twenty-four-hour supervision which she really needed.'

'When do you think that should have been?'

'When the baby was about a month old, that's when I first began to feel unhappy about it.'

In situations like this it is not easy to keep a fully balanced judgement. When listening to the mother one tends to see her viewpoint only : when it is the health visitor's turn your sympathies swing towards *her* as you realize just how heavy a burden the support of such a mother must be. A successful health visitor or social worker needs to be a paragon: she must be gentle and yet firm; sympathetic but not taken in by lies and evasions; intelligent but able to tune in to the less bright when necessary; able to give herself openly to the person she is dealing with so that they will respond equally openly, yet at the same time she must remain detached so that she does not become emotionally involved. On top of all that it would be desirable if she were available twenty-four hours a day seven days a week. Clearly no one can fill all these desiderata. Even the best-intentioned will sometimes be unwell or unhappy for personal reasons, and obviously no one can be on duty every minute of their lives.

Ways of coping with this particular problem will be examined later: for the moment we will take another look at the first mother we met, in Chapter 1, Mrs Jones, who would have agreed with the health visitor's comment here that the mother should have been admitted to a hospital for supervision. Mrs Jones said that she wished she had been made to go away to a residential hospital after her suicide attempt: 'For four years now they've talked about sending Paul and myself away . . . but nobody ever does anything: they're going to wait until I do something desperate. No, they couldn't force me to go away, I wasn't barmy enough for that, but in spite of the fact that I refused to go, really I wish they'd made me. Underneath it I really wanted to go. I kept trying to tell them how desperate I was. If only they'd said to me, you've got to go away for a week with Paul, no ifs or buts.'

Her health visitor told me that Mrs Jones had become hysterical at the thought of being sent away, and had refused so adamantly that finally they had given way to her and let her stay at home. At the time she had seemed to fear that it was all part of a plan to separate her from her son Paul. From these two mothers' remarks some of the helping agencies' problems can clearly be seen. How are they to know what would be best for the mother in the end? How are they to interpret what the

mother is actually saying behind the words she throws at them?
Mrs Jones' health visitor, a warm and sympathetic person, was
very attached to her and certainly had her trust, and yet she
did not penetrate through to the level at which Mrs Jones
wanted to be dominated. Probably Mrs Jones would never have
admitted such a desire except to someone such as myself who
was not in a position to have her sent away. Laws preventing
people being forcibly removed from their homes except in
cases of severe mental disturbance are obviously necessary:
everyone concerned with Mrs Jones was therefore acting
correctly in not insisting she went away when she appeared
determined not to go. Yet equally clearly she should have
gone.

Let us look at another case where the social services were
much criticized recently. 'Mr A—, Director of Social Services
for Y—, admitted today that with the advantage of hindsight
his department would probably have dealt differently with the
case of a boy aged two who died after being beaten by his
mother and stepfather. "This case emphasizes the dilemma
facing the social worker in trying to strike a balance between
the parents' rights and what is in the best interest of the child",
he said. The child, who had been returned to the parents only a
month earlier from foster parents, had his hair wrenched out
and his right arm pulled from its socket. Twice previously its
injuries, including a fractured leg, had been brought to the
attention of the welfare authorities.

'Mr A— said the boy was originally taken into care by the
welfare department with the agreement of the mother and the
stepfather. He added: "When they demanded his return we
had no real option because there appeared to be no evidence on
which we could proceed to assume parental rights under the
1938 [properly 1948] Children's Act." With hindsight, he said,
they could have handled the matter differently. There was provision in the 1969 Children and Young Persons Act for magistrates to make a child safety order if they were satisfied that
there had been neglect or ill-treatment and that the child was in
need of care and control. "We shall make better use of this

legislation in cases where child battering is suspected," he said.' (*The Times*, 1972.)

The 1969 Act is a very important one, and is still under-used. Official bodies do not change their ways without a great deal of internal turbulence, and it will be some time before all agencies fully realize they have more power now to separate children from their parents when necessary. Under the old 1948 Act the social workers in question had little choice but to return the two-year-old to his fate. One hopes that his death will not have been in vain and that social workers all over the country have learned from the case.

In this book certain criticisms of the various agencies working in this field will be discussed because time and time again I have found distrust and suspicion between them. Each group understands and therefore accepts its own difficulties, but is less tolerant of other people's inadequacies. The real problem is that there are many different ways of looking at battering and as many different ways of treating it, and it cannot be expected that all the groups, each of whom holds firmly to its own pet theories, will agree with each other.

First let us look at a few criticisms of the social services, and then we shall hear their reply. Social workers frequently complain about the police's behaviour; what do the police say about them? One woman Inspector, tough-spoken and knowing her rough area inside out, said, 'They're too middle-class, most of our social workers. They don't understand working-class language. They're communicating at different levels, and they don't realize it. They're very careful how they speak to these parents, they don't want to cause any offence, and the result is they don't get anywhere. I say, "Look here, Maisie, you've been stubbing your bloody fag-end out on this kid, haven't you!" and the odds are Maisie will admit it. I don't say it in an accusing way, just as a statement of fact, and they'll mostly take it that way. The old-style social worker might have come right out with it like that too, but she would have been *condemning*, and she'd have got nowhere either. You see, *they* know I know: they've been brought up all their lives to expect the coppers to move in if they've done wrong, and if they've bashed up their kids they bloody well know they've done wrong and they expect us to come in. But if the whole thing is hushed up and treated with kid gloves, and that's what keeps happening now, then these mothers are *more* disturbed, not less. It's not what they expected, and they don't know what to make of it. There's a cultural difference there, and your average social worker just doesn't realize how deep it goes.

'I went to see a woman I know a few months back : they live in a terrible state, really filthy – you can't imagine how it stinks. She'd been seeing her social worker a couple of times a week for about a year and they got on fine. But do you know all this woman could talk to me about? Her social worker's marriage problems! It seems they've spent half their sessions working over her marriage which was apparently in a disastrous state. "Look love," I said, "I don't give a bugger about your social worker's marriage, it's *yours* I'm worried about." Now maybe this social worker felt that by opening up this woman's mind to other people's troubles she was increasing her understanding or something, but to my mind what that woman really wanted was actual support, someone to roll up her sleeves and clean up her house for her, help her work out her money for her, get her life put straight, not tea and sympathy!'

Another police accusation I came across several times is that many social workers do not know their law well enough : there are many statutes controlling treatment of various aspects of child abuse, and not all workers are properly familiar with the correct processes of law. Repeatedly the police complain they are not told when an attack has taken place, and that the social workers are behaving incorrectly in not informing them. There is no doubt in my mind that most social workers place their loyalty to their clients first, well above any scruples about pre- cisely following the letter of the law. Obviously, in really vio- lent cases they have no choice, but for the rest, if they and the paediatrician concerned see eye to eye, the police will not be told what has happened. There is an important side effect to this : as one police officer said bitterly, 'It's no use your ringing up the Home Office to get statistics on the amount of baby battering – they don't have the faintest idea. Their figures are all wrong because they don't get told the half of it.'

Another frequent police complaint is that social workers are not trained investigators and often fail to discover vital facts because they only listen to the parent. 'The mother gives a thoroughly convincing story and the social workers and the doctors are taken in, but it may well be that the neighbours could give an entirely different story. Well, who's going to find this out, the social worker? No, they only listen to what the parent has to say. In this situation you need a thoroughly experienced policewoman to go and make enquiries among neighbours and relatives – find out who visits the house, and talk to them. Tradesmen, people like that – they often see things, hear things, and sometimes they present a very different picture to the one the mother gives. You need to know the truth if you're going to deal successfully with the parents : it's no good being taken in by them. That doesn't help anybody.

'Not only that, it queers our pitch for us. We go along, but it's too late. The mother or father have told their story several times, they've got it all tied up and we can't break it. It's impossible to get an admission under those circumstances – all the initiative is taken out of our hands. That sort of enquiry is none of the social workers' business.'

Obviously the basic attitudes here are entirely different. The social worker knows her clients well; perhaps has visited them over a period of years and is personally involved in the family's success or failure. Her primary interest is that the family works as a unit and that somehow it stays patched up and in a condition that allows it to continue to stick together. Police interference could mean the break-up of the family : the children might be removed or one of the parents imprisoned. In her terms this is a failure of her work over the years : it is natural therefore that she will resist this break-up for as long as she can convince herself it is safe to do so.

The police, on the other hand, look at what has happened from an outsider's point of view : 'We're here to protect, and

that means we protect the child every bit as much as we protect the parent. It's our *duty* to protect the child, and we
mustn't be hindered from doing so.' Without close cooperation
and a certain amount of give-and-take on interpretation of the
law on the part of the police, it is obvious that conflict is bound
to arise when two such different attitudes meet. Where such
cooperation does exist both sides have found their work made
both much easier and more rewarding.

Even in areas where progress has been made in this field it
takes time for all the problems to be ironed out, and certain
bitternesses linger. The word 'bitterness' is not over-emphatic :
many policemen and women I met are genuinely upset that
they are still expected to have no interests except in increasing
the number of people they can throw into jail. They resent the
image popularly thrust upon them : 'You get cheesed with it,'
(a woman police sergeant speaking) 'you only get called in at
the end when you can't do anything, and then you get nothing
but suspicion.' From another policewoman : 'It's very significant how all these deeply involved social workers become disin-
volved at the weekends. If it happens at the weekend *we* get it,
if it happens in the week we never see it, hear it, they just don't
want us to know about it.'

A few complaints were made by doctors, but these were
usually less severe. Some did feel that social workers ought to
bring the children along to them for examination much earlier,
and that their emotional attachments to the parents occasionally
meant a child's life was unnecessarily endangered while they
tried to sort out the parents' problems. A psychiatrist commented that social workers were necessarily 'amateur psychologists' and sometimes wrongly attempted to tackle mental
disturbances which were far beyond their capabilities. 'They
attend a lecture or two and imagine they know all about the
mind, but it's infinitely more complicated than that. It's a tricky
field, and it terrifies me to think of the danger of such parents
being worked on by some earnest, well-meaning amateur.'

Mrs Jones's health visitor had exactly the opposite comment
to make, however. At the time of Mrs Jones's attempted suicide

she had been extremely worried about her, and had contacted Mrs Jones's psychiatrist, telling her she felt her client was under particular stress at that time and that she feared something serious might happen. The psychiatrist reassured her, saying everything was going very well, and that there was no danger. Within two or three days Mrs Jones had tried to fling herself under a car. Again, both sides here were convinced that they knew her best, and in this particular instance it was the health visitor who was right. Similarly with the case of Mrs Brown who nearly strangled her little daughter Emma : here the health visitor had contacted both the GP and the psychiatric out-patients department to alert them, but in spite of that, the full seriousness of the situation did not seem to have been appreciated by them.

I shall give one last instance of a failure in the relationship between doctor, police and social worker. It is a typical story, not in points of detail, but in the way total lack of cooperation can result in exacerbating a situation. This particular case, as it turned out, was only a false alarm, but had the mother actually been battering her child the result could easily have been tragic. The paediatrician concerned is very interested in battered babies and if there is any cause at all for suspicion he always takes action : 'A young mother of about 22 with four children all under five brought one of them in because of some congenital defect or other. Now he also had a bruise on his forehead. I asked her how he'd got it and she said he'd fallen over. It seemed to me that, whatever was the truth of that bruise, he was a child who just might be at risk in view of his mother's situation. She had no husband and she was on social assistance, so there was a set up there that suggested to me he might be a baby at risk. Well, I asked the social workers to make a social history, but the mother disappeared from the hospital without the social workers having a chance to get it. Because of my anxiety about the child the hospital social worker rang the social worker of the borough, explained that Dr – wasn't calling it a battered baby but was worried about the general situation, and would they call on the family and see whether his anxieties were justified or not. The first thing that happened to that mother after she got home from the hospital was a visit by two uniformed policemen! What had happened was that as soon as the social workers of this borough got the message they rang the police with this really most ridiculously slender evidence, and asked them to make enquiries. Of course they found absolutely nothing to be suspicious about, and when the mother came back to hospital later for the child's treatment her language was pretty ripe, as you can imagine. You know: look, what the bloody hell have you done to *me*? I no sooner come to see you as a doctor than I've got a couple of policemen on my doorstep! Well, that's no way for people to think about their doctors is it? It happened because the particular borough which that mother came from has the principle that it would be condoning a crime if they don't inform the police about any baby battering whatsoever reported to them by a doctor. That's the trouble with rules, you see: if the junior person who takes the telephone message can't get in touch with his senior, and the rule says you must inform, then that's just what he does, regardless of the sense of it.'

The social services department of a nearby borough took the opposite view: they commented to me that the hospital at which that particular paediatrician worked 'had battered babies on their minds: that's all they ever seem to think of', with the clear implication that they considered the mild suspicions occasionally reported to them as a waste of their time. Most social workers will probably fall between these two extremes of reaction, but it can be seen that, whatever the official doctrine, when it comes to what action is taken in any particular case, everything depends on the local attitude.

I put some of these points of criticism to the Director of Social Services of a large London borough. His reaction was to dismiss them as being grossly biased. No doubt from his point of view he was absolutely right. His own borough is a wealthy one and he is able to pick and choose his staff: at weekends a skeleton telephone service is always maintained for those in need. Also, most important, the ratio of fully-trained social workers to as yet unqualified trainees in his borough is quite different from many other areas in Britain. 'Social workers are there to know the facts, no more no less than a policeman, and it's nonsense to suggest we go around with rose-tinted spectacles only looking for what would be attractive to find. We go to establish exactly what the thing between the mother and child is, has been and might be in the future. The police have got a thing about this – they argue up hill and down dale that local authorities should keep out of this and leave it to the police to get the parent and child away from each other. But a child who has been battered by a mother may have a far more robust and realistic future with that mother than anybody can guess, if she is given proper support. As for the legal side, without a shadow of a doubt social workers should know their law. The police are jaundiced about this too. It would be absolutely mad of us to let loose a social worker who doesn't know the law of the land. I'm sorry, but what you have here is the extraordinary acrimony that some police feel for what might be described as another line from their own. There can be no question that social workers know their law.'

Indeed there *can* be no question that a fully trained social worker knows his or her law. But there is one startling fact which is not generally known by the public at large, and that is that only approximately 30 per cent of our social workers are fully trained – that is to say they have had at least two years of some professionally accepted course in the social sciences. In this particular London borough trainee social workers are properly instructed and there is a sufficient number of fully trained workers available to supervise them adequately. But many other areas are less fortunate; often even less than a quarter of the available staff is fully trained.

Occasionally the situation may be that there is only one trained worker as group leader, with four or five untrained workers under him or her, two or three of whom may have just begun their new career and as yet are in almost total ignorance of anything at all to do with their work. A proportion of these will eventually be sacked as being unsuitable for the job, but meanwhile they may be the only contact with the social services which some stressed families will have. Many counties try to give a brief introductory course of a few weeks' duration to beginners before they start work, but not all counties can arrange even this. It can happen that a raw trainee will find himself working from 9 in the morning to 9 at night, desperately trying to cope with a case-load of fifty or more, yet lucky if he has an hour's supervision *a week*. Most of the time there will be no senior available to advise him, and he will have to make his own decisions entirely from his own commonsense and what bits of information he can pick up. This clearly is not the situation in this London borough, but unfortunately it is what is happening in many places throughout Britain. Is it then any wonder that a less than perfect service is being maintained, in spite of all the devoted and exhausting work being put in by over-stretched and underpaid teams of men and women?

A social worker being criticized for not picking up a potential case of battering in time may be one of the young trainees who, while suspecting that a certain mother was over-stressed, was never able to discuss it with her senior because other more pressing problems absorbed the whole of her weekly consultation. Or she may have been a thoroughly experienced senior who knew quite well that her client was badly stressed but her case-load of 140 clients made daily supportive visits impossible. Yet again, she may have been one of the social workers (who, unfortunately, do exist), who refuse to see what is under her nose. There are many records of child deaths which leave totally unexplained why the regular social worker chose to take no action, in spite of complaints from neighbours and relations. Whether through a mistaken belief that children should never be separated from their parents or whether through sheer obtuseness, such social workers remain blind to the agonies of the children they should be protecting. This type is probably fairly rare, but such ineptitude does undeniably exist.

It is no use saying that a battering mother ought to be visited every day if her social worker has too big a case load for it to be possible; it is no good saying the children must be taken to nursery schools to give the mother a break if there are no nursery schools available locally; it is no good talking blithely of community care and emotional support if the community doesn't in fact care enough to make sure these aids are available. And let us be clear about this – it *is* partly in the hands of the community; that is, you and me. The inhabitants of a borough elect their representatives to serve them on the local council, but what prospective councillor would stand a chance of being elected if he made his platform a large increase in the rates in order to give better support to those in need of help?

Each county is responsible for the distribution of the rates it collects. The money they raise for their local inhabitants is increased by a grant (known as the Rate Support Grant) from the Government which works out by a very complicated procedure how much of the total sum of money nationally available each individual county or county borough will receive. Some receive a higher percentage of their needs than others, but the national average is 58 per cent. The rest of the money must come from the rates. The intention of this variable grant is to ensure that poor counties are not made to suffer unfairly in comparison to their richer neighbours. How well does this work in practice? It is extremely difficult to tell, but certainly no one would claim that the system is yet perfect.

Let us look at some of the differences between various counties and boroughs. Kent, with a population of 1,373,290 has 187 social workers (these and the following figures are the latest available, taken from Local Health and Social Services Statistics, issued by the Institute of Municipal Treasurers and Accountants, 1971–2) while Essex, with a slightly smaller population of 1,196,840 has as many as 253 social workers. It cannot be that Kent's need is smaller, since it had 2,098 children in care in 1971, while Essex only had 1,299. If we compare the London borough of Camden (203,640 population) with the nearest comparably sized county, Huntingdon and Peterborough (population 205,780) we find that Camden has 102 social workers whereas Huntingdon only has 36. In this case Camden certainly has need of many social workers: while much of this borough is decidedly affluent, it also has many overcrowded areas of comparative poverty : 669 of its children were in care, or 18·3 out of every 1,000 children under 18. Huntingdon had 339 children in care, a mere 5·3 out of every 1,000 of the children under 18 in the county.

The Home Office National Statistics for March 1971 show that the average number of children in care in England per 1,000 of the population under 18 is 6·5. London's extra need may be gauged by Camden's figure, or even more so by that for Kensington and Chelsea (24·1) or Tower Hamlets (28·4). Many London boroughs feel that their special difficulties (higher rates of pay to their workers, costs of accommodation, etc., plus the inevitable problem caused by the high density of population per square mile, etc.) are not sufficiently taken into consideration when the Rate Support Grant is distributed by the Government. Camden, for example, receives a grant of only 32 per cent (25 per cent in real terms according to their reckoning) as against the national average of 58 per cent.

Obviously this whole problem of state intervention is very complicated, and behind all the arguments lie two main questions. If the Government were to take over all financial responsibility would they then dictate how the money should be spent? And second, if local councils do not want state dictation, are they prepared instead to demand a considerable rise in the rates from the people they have been elected to represent and will the public accept such a demand? One or other of these two things will probably have to happen if sufficient resources are to be made available to cope with all the ever-increasing demands made upon the social services.

The amount of money raised by different councils varies incredibly. Let us look at the product of the penny rate for the areas already mentioned (the penny rate is a *measure* of relative rateable resources of an area – it is useful for comparative purposes). In 1971 one old penny on the rates of Kent would have brought in £576,947, while the figure for Essex was very similar, £575,864 : clearly, therefore, Kent's money is being allocated differently from that of Essex. Camden's penny rate would have raised £340,614 : Kent and Essex, each with a population nearly seven times the size of Camden's, raised not quite twice as much. More directly, Huntingdon and Peterborough, which we earlier compared with Camden as being of similar size, raised only £82,349 as against Camden's £340,614.

This is not the place to go any further into such details : every county has its own peculiarities and the above figures have been quoted purely to show the discrepancies between the rates levied in different areas. Clearly, the problem of settling the amount of rates to be paid by any particular area is one purely for the experts, and political considerations ought to play no part in the decision, yet obviously they must do. There are so many variables : does a county collect only a small sum from its rates because most of its inhabitants are poor and cannot pay, or because they are rich and there is little need of social services? Should an overcrowded borough like some of the London ones collect even higher rates from those of its inhabitants lucky enough to own their own homes to help care for their less fortunate fellow-inhabitants, or should the Government bear in mind that many of those needing aid will have come into London from other areas and perhaps ought therefore to be supported by extra Government grants rather than by the local residents?

These few pages only brush the surface of the problem, and eventually some more equable scheme will probably be worked out. Meanwhile, conditions among social workers are not equal. Some are grossly overworked, some only mildly so. It is certainly safe to say that none are under-worked.

To answer some of the criticisms about social workers I can do no better than quote from a long incensed letter sent to me by a man of 35 who decided to take up social work as a career. He has now successfully finished his first year, and has been accepted for a two-year university training course. In case any-one should think he is exaggerating or comes from a uniquely bad county, I might preface his letter by adding that I was assured by the British Association of Social Workers that unfortunately the problems which he describes so vividly are only too familiar to social workers in many parts of the country.

'Before I applied for a post, I read a lot and I asked around.

"You are bound to be thrown in the deep end", I was told. "With staff shortages, it's inevitable. But make sure you don't take a job anywhere where they are offering you *less* than one hour's supervision a week. You'll be very lucky to get more."

'I was amazed that a total newcomer with no experience could be let loose on an unsuspecting public with so little guidance and instruction. I assumed it must mean I'd only be given simple cases at first, but when I got my first job I found the office grossly under-staffed and cases were pouring in. For many clients it was me or nothing. And the cases weren't at all simple : I had to tackle anything that turned up. It's very un-pleasant for a senior to have to turn down a case and say to a client in need – sorry, we're too short-staffed to help – even when he knows he's already pushing himself to the limit. So often they take on more than the group can really handle.

'On my first day I was given a caseload of about 30. Within three months the number was soaring up and by seven months it was well over the hundred mark. It's true that if I hadn't shown a reasonable degree of aptitude I wouldn't have been given so many. But remember I was still an untrained beginner.

'I can just hear the indignant mutterings from higher levels that of course he had seniors on tap to ask for help whenever he needed it, that there's always a senior on duty. Well, yes, if you're good at lassoeing a fast runner. The truth is if you're wise you only call for help on something really tough. Seniors are pretty thin on the ground and, like anyone else under great pressure, they are liable to get killed in motor accidents, com-mit suicide or just drop out into easier jobs. Then you'd be on your own. So you watch it.

'Unfortunately the problem doesn't stop there. Let's skip the 60-hour week with no overtime pay (I'm paid for a 35 hour week – recently we had a "rise" in the form of a shorter week : office closing 4.15 Friday instead of 5.15, which as one is never finished before 6 was utterly meaningless) and the overcrowded office where you fight for desk and telephone in sordid condi-tions which no commercial firm competing for labour would ever get away with. But just stop and think about some of the

effects of the Seebohm Report which resulted in the reorganization of the social services. Instead of specialists, there is a team
of generic social workers who are all equally equipped to deal
with all problems; one social worker per family, seeing their
problems as a whole instead of a constant succession of various
"helpers" trooping in and out; social workers working as a team,
helping each other for the benefit of the client. It all sounded
marvellous to me before I started. I still think it's a good idea.
But does anyone realize the toll it's taking of the quality of the
social work which is being done right now while the scheme is
getting under way? Does anyone really appreciate what it's like
to come in new to the whole game and have to learn about the
facilities available and the pile of legislation – the Children's
Acts, the new laws on juvenile offenders, the mental health
regulations, new provision for the Chronic Sick and Disabled,
divorce laws, legal aid provisions, regulations for nursery
schools and child minders, Family Income Supplement, Supple-
mentary Benefit? (You must be able to advise the client on
what he's entitled to and how to get it.)

'The social worker trying to give patient sympathy, help, understanding and guidance to a baby batterer needs all his facul-
ties on the alert to judge just how long he dare leave that child
in that situation, to avoid breaking up the family. But perhaps
that same day he has been trying desperately to find help to
keep an 80-year-old in his own home because with heart-touch-
ing independence the old codger refuses to lose his freedom
and go into an old people's home. He has also had to remove a
fighting mad and very deluded schizophrenic to a mental hospital (and remember that though the doctor and psychiatrist
may be called in it is the social worker's responsibility for deciding she must go. And *he* takes the can back if she sues him
later to prove wrongful admission). He may also have taken
little Johnny who's in care out for tea on his birthday (because
his relatives won't) and then dropped in to see Harry, adoles-
cent, brain damaged, doubly incontinent and very aggressive
with it. Harry's mother may have phoned him up three times
already that week to demand Harry be "put away" because she

can't stand it. But there isn't anywhere yet for Harry, though he's been on the waiting list for four years. And that morning the Jones family had turned up in his office with twenty carrier bags of possessions and nowhere to go, evicted from a tied cot-tage with no relatives to turn to for help – and the local council housing manager just doesn't want to know. It's not unusual to have eight interviews such as these in a day and when he gets home there's a pile of paperwork still to be done. What sort of concentration and sensitive support is he going to be able to give the potential battering mum in the few minutes he can spare her?

'Then there's the team. I'd imagined I'd be the one beginner in a team of trained, skilled workers. Instead it's the other way round – there's only one *trained* person, and the rest of us are all beginners. His training was pre-Seebohm, so as he was trained in mental health he's having to learn the child care side. Most of the seniors are in the same boat. You have to play it by ear, and most of the time you play it alone.

'You try hard not to think about the visits you haven't made; the help you couldn't give because you hadn't enough know-ledge or time; the doctors, health visitors, medical social work-ers, local councillors and relatives of clients who've "got at" you during the day with little sympathy or understanding or tact, because they just don't understand why you haven't got things done. (And they don't really want to understand . . . it might mean another penny on the rates!) But you don't succeed.

'In all the cases I have read in the papers where say a child has been battered or an old lady has died unattended, no one has ever put the local authority's point of view. It is never quoted that their social workers are probably doing a 60–80 hour week (if it's a big city) plus emergency duty (all night, all weekend on call), so that they just cannot watch everything all the time. The public pays its money and gets the service it pays for (and a bloody sight more). The social services are whipping-boys, while the better-off ratepayers go and build their swim-ming pools and tennis courts, and buy their second car and second colour TV without a twinge of conscience. I'm *not* exaggerating – I see it around me all the time. I'm *sick* of being berated by middle-class businessmen in very cushy circumstances (when I'm visiting them at 8 or 9 p.m.) because I haven't managed to conjure up an Old People's Home for their mother-in-law whom they want to get rid of.

'Why the hell do you go on with it? Because you believe it *must* change, must get better as more people are trained and qualified. *If* universities expand to provide enough training courses, *if* local authorities (which really means the ratepayers) decide to spend the money, and *if* area directors stop trying to push all the dirt under the carpet and pretend it's all lovely on their patch.'

Health visitors, while as overworked as social workers, at least have the advantage of a proper medical training. They are all state registered nurses with midwifery training plus a year's further academic training. Indeed, they often complain that although they may have far more professional expertise than a social worker, it is only the Local Authority social worker or NSPCC social worker who is empowered to make the decision whether or not to apply for a Care Order to remove a child from its family. Health visitors have a statutory duty to visit all newly-born babies, and so are in a particularly advantageous position to watch for battering. However, to avoid constant repetition and qualifications I have frequently used the phrase 'social worker' to cover both health visitors and social workers. This is a practice common among nearly everyone I spoke to, so that in any particular quotation a doctor or policeman may actually be referring to social workers or health visitors when he uses the phrase 'social worker'. Understandably this is a source of irritation to health visitors, but since there is no general term I am forced also to follow this practice when I refer to the whole group of workers concerned with the family.

Chapter 5

The social worker and the NSPCC

If in the last chapter I seem to have concentrated on the problems rather than on the many successes of the social services, it is because the social services lie at the heart of the success or failure of any scheme to help battering parents, and it is essential that the difficulties they face should be understood by everyone. Social workers and health visitors are in the best position to recognize a potentially dangerous situation.

There is one important advantage of early intervention which is becoming clear to workers : parents take more kindly to help given at this period and are more influenced by it than when they have actually injured their children, as their guilt often makes them highly defensive. As a result they may not admit to any problems at all, whereas earlier they might have been only too glad to talk to someone.

The social worker needs to be very skilful, however, if her intervention is to be successful. Ray Castle writes in *78 Battered Children: A Retrospective Study:*

it was the authors' general impression that actions which added to existing family tension precipitated further battering. . . The rebattering incidence of 60 per cent in a sample of cases known to a protective agency does not compare favourably with the estimate that 25–50 per cent are rebattered in the absence of any intervention. . . The findings suggest that multiplicity of workers and overfrequent observation of battering families can increase family stress, and a type of supervision of a family which is limited to an anxious watchfulness without specific treatment goals is not in the child's interest.

One attitude *not* to take was illustrated by the following authoritarian social worker. 'I told the mother of the allegations against her and her cohabitee. She immediately denied the allegations . . . I asked the mother if I could look at the child. I warned her of the seriousness of the offence and that I should want to return to see the children to assure myself and my Society that they were not being ill-treated or neglected in any way.' Such an attitude could increase the guilt and anxiety of the mother dangerously, although the case-worker, no doubt revolted by the mother's attack, probably felt herself very self-controlled not to be openly blaming.

However, thanks partly to the results of the NSPCC's research, such attitudes are growing rarer, and those involved are being given helpful advice on how to approach such parents. In *Midwife and Health Visitor* (1969) Carolyn Okell said:

Direct interest in the infant should be avoided by the worker and the focus of the visit must be the parent, otherwise she will begin to feel frozen out by both the worker and the child. Probably the most precious gifts one can give them are time, sympathy, empathetic listening and attention, for they have an aching void of rejection. This may sound hard to those who are specially concerned with the infants' health and safety, but it is becoming apparent that a multiplicity of workers and overfrequent observation of battering families can increase family stress.

Joan Court wrote in the *Midwives Chronicle* in 1970:

Our basic aim must be to try to give the mother an experience of the mothering that she herself has never had. Try to be a kind, wise and understanding mother to her. It will not be easy. Whenever you visit she is likely to be out. She will not keep appointments nor turn up at the clinics. The failure of love in her background came at the stage before she could talk, and before she begins to trust you she will unconsciously be looking for evidence of your caring in a non-verbal form. To call persistently, even when she is out on many occasions, is a proof to her that you care enough to do it. . . Like all good mothers you should concentrate on listening rather than talking. A sympathetic listener makes people feel worthwhile. . . It may make you feel better if you focus on the child but it will make the mother feel worse, and the child may be at the receiving end of a burst of pent-up guilt and subsequent anger when you have gone. Concentrate on the mother and make her feel better, and she will be better with the child. If possible, try to be more on demand than you have time to be with most people. If the mother knows that she can contact you when she is feeling at odds with herself or the children, you may be able to avert an attack. . . Beware of appeals to you for advice. These appeals mask a fear of domination springing from feelings towards past demands, and anxiety to comply because they fear yet another rejection, and distress because they will not make the grade and be made to suffer for it. As children they were made to express gratitude when they did not feel it, and who wants help at that price?

What happens when a social worker decides a child is in danger? If she feels an attack is imminent, then she will try to get a care order placed on the child. If the application is successful the child will normally be placed either in a foster home or in a reception centre, a residential nursery or some other children's home until the family situation is eased. Knowing when to return the child home is the result of many years' experience. As one doctor put it: 'This is where social expertise comes in, your expert social worker knows the right time. It's very easy to know when you must separate them, but it's obviously trickier putting them back together again. I suppose it's when you realize the heat has gone out of the situation – you can't define the moment, it's a question of very many little points, adding them all up until you know the right time has come.' Juliet Berry wrote: 'One mother said towards the end of treatment, "I'm listening to my little girl the way you listen to me. She's a real person to me now and I enjoy her . . ." '

But the situation is still fraught with danger, even if all seems well on the surface. Estimates vary as to how many children have already had some form of medical treatment for injury before major damage is done, but some put it as high as 50 per cent. Ray Castle reports in the *Retrospective Study* (1969) that at least two in every five children had received medical attention before the attack detailed in the study, and of those discharged home three in every five required it again.

Some areas invoke the help of a psychiatrist to decide when a child may be returned, others depend on local social workers, and yet others on the considered opinion of a special committee consisting of a variety of workers – doctors, social workers, NSPCC, health visitors, etc. Where people's emotions are involved any method must remain hit-and-miss, and it is difficult to see how mistakes can be avoided as long as it is felt important to return a child to his home as soon as possible. Certainly many returned children will be rebattered, even killed, until general understanding of the phenomenon of baby battering is considerably increased.

A Home Office analysis of reports from medical officers of health and children's officers throughout the country shows that one of the following plans for the child discharged from hospital is usually adopted. Either the child is returned home with planned help to the family, or he is received into care at the parents' request in order to relieve them from strain in a difficult family situation. Alternatively the child may be committed to care by a court order, or supervised in his own home by order of a court.

'In practice there is frequently a worrying and frustrating stalemate, because while it seems against the child's interest to return home, the parents will not agree to reception into care and there appears to be insufficient evidence to enable care proceedings to be brought.

'Where a child does return home on discharge from hospital, steps have to be taken to minimize the risk of further injuries to the child and this is given prominence in the reports. The problem of protecting the child within its own home is part of the larger social problem that is being tackled by the unified social services departments, in cooperation with the community health services. Great importance is attached to day nurseries, nursery schools, playgroups and family supportive work.'

So once again, responsibility is thrown back on to the social services. Time, patience, knowledge and continuous support from their peers and superiors is all the average social worker needs to enable him to cope with the situation, but we have seen how scarce the first and last of these can be in some over-stressed areas. Yet each family must be guarded and watched over individually. As one Director of Social Services said of his large borough, 'A social worker who knows four streets intimately is worth five times as much as a social worker who drifts right across the face of the borough, fingering his or her car keys anxious to get on to the next port of call.'

Given the present lack of resources, what can be done now to ease the situation? One possible answer is 'mothering aids'. In America this system has been tried, with successful results. Recently Dr Kempe talked about his 'lifeline' in Colorado. 'There are three phone numbers, one of which is always ready to take a call, seven days a week, twenty-four hours a day. And moments of crisis tend to come not between 9 and 5, Monday to Friday, but at any time. One has to be prepared to take the phone and chat about anything that comes up – to provide, in fact, a link that will prevent the hitting out at the child. The precedent in your country has been the successful use of the Samaritans for the prevention of suicides. It doesn't matter what label is applied to the people at the end of the telephone – they can be health visitors, social workers, doctors, or they can be the mothering aids or foster grandmothers we use in Colorado who are not professionally trained except that they've had the best of all training, that is to say they've had a warm, loving giving mother or father and hopefully they have been a good, loving mother or father themselves. They are from all walks of life, they are anything at all in terms of their financial background. But they have in common a generous desire to help another adult. This is not easy. It's been our feeling that very few mothering aids can handle the kind of support that is needed by more than just perhaps two battering families.'

Reactions to the idea of mothering aids vary. One doctor felt that 'there is a great danger that the untrained mothering aid will start mothering the child, and if they do that the child will be in even greater danger. To pick suitable people would be a matter of the greatest difficulty. If somebody says I want to do good to somebody, how can I do it? and they get put on this job, they are likely to start organizing the situation. What you really want is a rather large mothering figure, not very bright, who will sit down and chat for hours, and if the child comes around she'll just ignore it, pat it on its head and say, run away and play. She needs to mother the *mother*, not the child.'

On the other hand a police surgeon who in the course of his duties has seen many middle-aged women brought in for shop-lifting or drunken behaviour, said 'One group I can think of in particular who might help are professional wives whose children have grown up. They feel themselves rejected. Take a doctor's wife who might well have been a nursing sister before she married, and acted as her husband's receptionist or nurse before she had children. Now her husband is in a group practice or doing very well and there's his wife, children grown up, nothing to do, bored stiff, but she doesn't want to do a full time job. Some of these women start shoplifting, or begin to drink too much, and there you are. We see it time and time again. No one takes any notice of them until they land up here, then their husbands come running, the family solicitor comes round, and the family doctor; for the first time for years they're the centre of attention, mum's in the nick. Now many of them are of good intelligence, and good heart, and I think it would solve a lot of problems all round if they could be used in this way. Otherwise their lives revolve round coffee mornings and afternoon teas and a few nips of gin here and there to keep the boredom away. They're wasted, and they know it, and I think they'd jump at the chance to help if it was organized properly.'

It certainly seems to me that recruitment on a large scale of such women (and why not men too?) would go a long way to help social workers cope with the burden of regular visits. Obviously choosing such women would be very difficult – do we take Kempe's word for it that the helpers can be of any back-ground, or would it be best if they came from a similar back-ground to the person who is to be aided? Would it be best if they were bright or if they were not very quick-witted? Would the social worker be the one to choose which helper should be allocated to which family, or would it be a case of first come, first served? Whatever the problems involved, they should not be allowed to prevent this idea from taking root. After all, someone who offers to help but seems unsuitable for this particular job can probably be channelled tactfully into other fields, such as looking after old people, or walking with or reading to the blind.

What do the parents themselves think of such an idea? Mrs Jones, whose story was told in Chapter 1, had several comments to make. We had been talking about the embarrassment of having to ask for everything you want from the Social Security people, and she had instanced the fact that she would like twin beds, but that it was useless to ask since her double bed was still in perfectly good condition. It will be remembered that her husband was impotent, and she therefore found it acutely stressful to lie next to him night after night, each trying not to touch the other by accident. Twin beds, she felt, would help them both to put the situation out of their minds to a certain extent.

I asked her if she was on sufficiently intimate terms with anyone whom she could ask for such a thing. 'Not really. I would ask my health visitor, I suppose, if we had long enough to chat like you and I have done today, but she can't stay all that long, and somehow I never get around to that sort of thing. I don't want her to think I'm begging, you see. She does so much for me already. It seems to me if there were some sort of liaison person who'd come round once every two or three months, not as a regular social worker but someone you'd get to know well enough to be able to ask something like that. I mean these people who go to all these church meetings, or the Women's Guilds, that sort of thing, wouldn't they love to have something to do like that? If they came round to see you and said, "Well, now, is there any way I can help? Don't be frightened to say," then you could say to them, "Well, the *sheets* are getting thin" – I mean, naturally you wouldn't bleed them, but things like that aren't taken into account, sheets and blankets wearing out, all that kind of thing.'

Later when we talked about stress, Mrs Jones said she felt particularly upset just before her period started. One solution we discussed would be for any pre-school child to have the automatic right to go to a day nursery for the entire day during those important three or four days. If it were done carefully –

the same nurse allocated to the same children each month, for example – it could save much injury, even lives. Mrs Jones also commented, 'Another thing that would help, I'd love to have someone round for a chat at that time. I get so tense and worked up I scream and shout, and I'm not placid at all ... and Paul comes in for more pushes and hits. If someone could come then and have a chat with me, it would help. You know, say how you are feeling, how are things going? Once you've spoken to somebody you don't feel so... If you know someone's going to call in, you feel better straight away. But it must be regular, someone you've got to know and like.' And later, talking about stress and the mothers' need to get away from their families for a while, or better still to go off for a few days with their husbands (something most middle-class parents manage occasionally) she said, 'Now if you could get a temporary mum, a motherly sort of woman to come in so you'd get a long weekend away somewhere, you'd have a break and you'd appreciate your home and children more. But when you don't get that break it gets worse and worse and you can't do anything about it. But it's got to be a woman you can trust – you've got to know your home's being run properly, or you wouldn't relax, it would be no good to you at all.'

It might be objected that all this would mean cosseting such families to a ludicrous extent. But let us look at some of the suggestions more closely. It is a proven fact that more crime is committed and more accidents sustained by women during their pre-menstrual period. As far as I know no one has systematically investigated this specifically with regard to battering, but from general observation I feel certain that the curve of attacks on children also would rise dramatically during that time. I feel equally certain that if it were not a biological fact about women which is over-laden with antique myths and sexual taboos that we were talking about, but some less embarrassing factor, more research into pre-menstrual tension would have been undertaken by now.

When I mentioned the idea of special help to potential or actual battering mothers during this particular time to a very sympathetic doctor much involved in these cases, however, even he smiled as though I had made some totally impossible suggestion. In a male-dominated society such uniquely female events must inevitably cause some embarrassment, but surely nowadays this can be overcome and the situation looked at squarely. If women really are more likely to attack at a certain time in the month (and in the majority of cases menstruation is predictable within two or three days) then doesn't it make sense that they should be given particular help at those times? The idea of having women's menstrual charts filed away somewhere in an office is certainly odd, but with enough willingness all round some effective system of visiting could be arranged, along with a flexible nursery scheme where any pre-school children at risk could be looked after for the vital few days a month. Hundreds of injuries annually could almost certainly be averted, and many lives saved.

At present social workers would not be able to undertake this extra work, nor would they necessarily be the right people to do it. Visits from a woman with a few spare hours a week and no overtones of officialdom would be a great blessing to many lonely mothers, particularly those in new estates or in the obnoxious tower blocks which themselves are responsible for so much stress. Some social workers might at first object to the idea of this untrained voluntary labour, but once they realized that none of their own professional jobs were being taken over, would they not welcome it? It is true that when many of them joined the service they probably saw themselves in just that role, the role of the pleasant helper relieving stress by gentle wise talk and kind action, but the present truth is that they just do not have the time. At long as this is so it is absurd not to make positive energetic efforts to enrol the many thousands of women who do not want full-time jobs, who are not trained for a career but who do not want to go back to the secretarial work or whatever it was they did for a few years before marriage.

The work could be entirely voluntary, or there could be payment: Kempe pays his workers a small hourly sum. It is not only middle class women whose willingness could be tapped. Many women used to go out doing other people's housework, mostly to earn a few extra shillings, but sometimes partly to have the opportunity of talking to someone else and spending an hour or two in a different house. Few women nowadays are prepared to wash somebody else's floors just for money, but might not many ordinary women be delighted to come for a small but useful fee to talk to and befriend people like themselves? Possibly they could also occasionally help with a little housecleaning, but primarily they would be there as friends, not as employees.

The small sums involved would easily be recovered from the money saved later in medical care. A battered child costs the nation a great deal of money. Imagine the costs involved: extra social workers will be needed, and ambulance drivers, policemen, general practitioners, paediatricians, nurses, surgeons, intensive care units, X-rays, medicines, psychiatric treatment for the parents, possibly imprisonment with financial support for the remaining family, after-care, foster parents, repeated hospital visits for the child, and a future expectation of further costs as the disturbed child grows up into adulthood.

To say preventive care cannot be afforded on economic grounds is demonstrably nonsense: it is only a rationalization of the attitude which still bedevils the entire field of medical care. One day, perhaps, it will be realized that it is better to prevent an illness than to patch up the bits afterwards. Less interesting, perhaps, from a medical point of view; but rather pleasanter for the patient.

Another factor of great help to social workers would be closer cooperation between all those involved in caring for any particular family. Mrs Jones's health visitor had these comments to make: 'I told you about how just before her attempted suicide I was worried that Mrs Jones might do something serious, but that her psychiatrist just didn't want to know. She kept saying it's quite all right, it's all in hand. As the "expert", she was certain she knew best. Then again, the social worker who looks after Mrs Jones's husband is not from the borough, he's blind himself and comes from another organization for the blind. He's never had any proper social work training at all. Now, none of us ever meet to discuss the situation. I *know* I know Mrs Jones better than her psychiatrist does: I've known her for years now, and see her several times a week. Her psychiatrist sees her half an hour a week at most. As for Mr Evans, as I said, he's blind and very much on the husband's side, he only sees *his* point of view. So you see, that family gets three different lots of advice, from three totally different sources looking at their problems in three different ways. It's ridiculous. We ought all to get together periodically and talk about the case. Yes, I suppose I might be able to arrange meetings with Mr Evans, but I doubt if the psychiatrist would come along. Not if *I* tried to arrange it, anyway, I'm only a Health Visitor, and she's busy, and she'd probably think I was being pushy!'

It is generally accepted now that one agency should have prime responsibility for a family and that all others cooperate fully: Kempe has stressed this time and again. As we have already seen the NSPCC has come to the same conclusion; failure in communication between different agencies can result in the death of a child. Does it not follow that whoever is most frequently in contact with the family should be at the centre of the care of the family: no matter how professionally superior others involved in the case may happen to be, that person ought to be consulted or at least informed directly about anything that affects the family under her care.

Mrs Jones had something to say on the subject of cooperation also. (If at this point the reader is beginning to wonder if I have invented the ubiquitous Mrs Jones may I assure him that Mrs Jones is very much alive, under another name of course.) Her revolutionary suggestion was that the parents themselves ought to be involved in these meetings – not to be talked *at*, but to join in as equal members of the group. 'I think that in cases like mine, where they know Paul was at risk and still is to a certain degree, I think that the psychiatrist, the social workers and myself should get together from time to time and try to find solutions to the home problem. Not all done behind my back, the way it is at present. They all see you individually, they talk to you very nicely, very sympathetically, but behind your back you'd be surprised what goes on. They all discuss you, and you've got no privacy. Well, I don't want to be just a case they talk about, *I* want to know what's going on, I want to be in on what they're deciding.'

Obviously such a suggestion will cause horror amongst many, but I am sure that Mrs Jones is not alone in feeling upset that 'they' know all about her and plan her life 'behind her back' just as though she were a paper figure in a file rather than a live human being. If Mrs Jones, who is lucky to have a particularly pleasant health visitor, feels like this, then others less fortunate may suffer an even greater sense of humiliation. Since it is unlikely to be expressed openly, workers can only guess at it and try to alleviate it as much as possible.

Another important point is that many of these families will need constant support throughout their entire period of child-rearing. This means they should be able to call on someone at any time of the day or night for possibly years on end. Clearly one social worker alone cannot undertake such a responsibility, particularly as such families can be extremely demanding, sometimes excessively so. That such consistent support does work, however, has been proved in Colorado and, closer home, by the National Society for the Prevention of Cruelty to Children.

The various references throughout this book to the NSPCC's Battered Child Research Department might have given the erroneous impression that the Department is devoted purely to clinical research, producing statistics and giving good advice. In fact as Ray Castle, the head of the Department, says, ' "Clinical research" implies treatment, because you can't do clinical research without having a group of families actually involved in treatment.' At present twenty-six families are being assisted by the Department and though they are in a sense the raw material of its studies, as far as the staff is concerned they are above all clients and friends.

The NSPCC has followed the same basic pattern of treatment as that used in Denver, Colorado. However, there are differences. Ray Castle points out that the American team primarily consists of medical personnel working within the hospital setting, whereas the NSPCC research team is working in the community and using the same medical resources which are available to ordinary social workers. This he feels is not only more realistic, but it is the best possible way of finding out exactly what current deficiencies must be corrected.

The two primary aspects of the Department's work are to study the problem of baby battering in depth and to examine various methods of treatment. The practical experience and knowledge they have gained in their work with the families has already been used to help set up a *treatment unit* (as opposed to a research centre) in Manchester in 1973 and a second one in Leeds in 1974. The Department has very recently been replaced by a National Advisory Centre, which will considerably extend the facilities already offered by the Department to other workers in the field.

Perhaps the most important result in their work is that, owing to the publicity they have gained since 1968 when they first began, more cases of battering are being brought to them at an early stage, both as referrals from a variety of sources and as direct approaches from the parents themselves. Both studies which they have since produced (*78 Battered Children: A Retrospective Study*, 1969; and *A Study of Suspected Child Abuse*, 1972) were fully reported in the press, frequently accompanied by sympathetic articles describing their work, so there can be few people who have not heard of the syndrome, however vague their appreciation might be of what it is all about. Parents who previously would not have dreamed of admitting their punitive desires to anyone at all, let alone to some official, are now beginning to see themselves as people in need of help and a few are even able to ask for that help. Out of a total of 292 referrals to the NSPCC in 1970, 32 were from the parents of the child themselves.

A comparison between the two studies of the source of referrals is interesting, although because of the different methods of collecting information used one must be careful not to make too much of it. (The *Retrospective Study* used information already gained during the ordinary course of the NSPCC's work during the period June 1967–June 1968, whereas the questionnaire cards sent out in 1970 for the second study were specially designed for use by the Research Department.) 'There was an increase in the number of parents referring themselves for help and in the number of referrals from Health Visitors. There continued to be a very low rate of referrals from General Practitioners (7 out of 292). As might be expected, the more seriously injured children were, in the main, referred by hospitals.'

Altogether three times as many cases of baby battering were referred to the NSPCC during 1970 as during the earlier period, the greatest increase coming from the referrals of moderately injured children of whom there were eight times as many as in the *Retrospective Study* sample. 'The authors [of the 1972 study] would suggest from these findings that the considerable increase in publicity and education on the subject of battered children has led to an increased awareness of the syndrome. It would seem unlikely there has been an actual increase in incidence. The findings indicate that the popularity of the NSPCC as a treatment agency for cases of suspected abuse has grown. . . .'

One might feel there is some anomaly in the very existence of a privately-financed body such as the NSPCC in a welfare state. But not only do they exist, they are the only organization in the United Kingdom carrying out research into the battered baby syndrome. There are many individuals devoting much of their time to this subject but this can only be as a part of their work as paediatrician, social worker, police superintendent or whatever. It has been left to the NSPCC to pioneer Britain's first and only research and treatment centres but they cannot afford to build many more such treatment units unless they receive substantial increases in financial backing. The Government, which at the time of writing gives them no monetary aid at all, is however, duly grateful for the task they have taken on. Sir Keith Joseph, when Secretary of State for Social Services (he once remarked 'we seem to have created a difficult social soil in which to grow families'), said at an NSPCC meeting, 'the more we look at this catalogue of misery the more it is mad to contemplate that the State can tackle it all – it cannot', and was clearly thankful that 'a quarter of the total number of child referrals in England and Wales come through the NSPCC and are handled to a greater or less extent by the NSPCC'.

However, there are some advantages in being independent. Providing its Central Executive Committee approves, the NSPCC is free to allocate its financial resources in the cause of research as it sees fit without any question of governmental interference, which might not be the case if Government money were forthcoming on any large scale. Another important advantage of its independent status is that the NSPCC has always regarded information given to it as confidential and promises anonymity to anyone reporting their suspicions about a neighbouring child who seems to cry too much or of a family where they sense something is wrong : such informants will not find themselves forced into court as reluctant witnesses. This is a very important assurance to many people, particularly to those who would feel bringing in the police to be a class betrayal.

I have occasionally heard mild complaints that the NSPCC situation is so atypical that its value is limited. It is true that each worker only has an average of eight to nine cases to look after (the treatment centres outside London have ten to eleven cases) but it must be remembered that not only is a higher ratio of worker/client needed because research is also involved, but that every one of these cases is potentially highly dangerous, unlike most of those an ordinary social worker has to deal with. It is also true that even if vast sums of money were suddenly allocated to the social services to improve child care alone, it is unlikely that there would be enough willing people of the right calibre available for training to provide a nationwide service of a similar type, and there would certainly be nothing like a sufficient number of trained social workers immediately available. Nevertheless, the NSPCC's example provides a blueprint of excellence which an ordinary overworked social worker can

attempt to follow within the limits imposed by the usual lack
of resources.

The original aim of the NSPCC team was to attempt to
'change the patterns of interaction at times of mounting stress
so that the parents will turn to the worker rather than the baby
for satisfaction of their own needs'. Such an act of trust probably implies a background of more time given to the individual client than the average social worker can spare but perhaps
if during her weekly/fortnightly visits she frequently suggested
to a suspected potential batterer that she would always welcome phone calls about any problem, without ever suggesting
the real reason for her concern, a stressed mother might make
such a call at a time of crisis even without a really close relationship first having been established.

The excellent relationship between the Battered Child Research Department staff and the families is the result of
thoughtful and continuous care. All pre-school children of the
clients are welcomed to the day nursery : if they cannot easily
walk the distance or the mothers don't always get around to
bringing them, they will be fetched by car. Sometimes a particularly depressed mother will not be out of bed when the car
calls and then without any suggestion of censure the worker
will dress the children and see they have their breakfast at the
nursery. The mother is therefore relieved of the strain of their
presence during the day and may go out to work or stay at
home or do whatever she wants.

If she feels like company she is made welcome at the nursery,
where a perpetually steaming kettle and plates of sandwiches
are always available in a comfortable sitting room. Some take
advantage of this and often come in for a chat and a cup of tea,
while others rarely put in an appearance. Behind this warm
smile of welcome there is the solid fact that twenty-four hours
a day, seven days a week, somebody is always on duty at the
end of a telephone. Every parent is allocated her own primary
social worker but they all know the rest of the team so that if
their primary worker is not available there is always another
person within reach whom they know and trust.

Since the Department began its clinical research programme, no child of a family referred has received serious physical reinjury. There have been occasional minor bruises, but nothing that cannot be seen any day on normal children. No doubt a few heavy-handed slaps have been administered as well, some of which might have resulted in bruising, but nothing worse has occurred; set against a normal rebattering rate (estimates vary, but at least 60 per cent seems to be an expected average) this is a remarkable record. Obviously these first few years have not been without their times of crisis, but these have been overcome. Most of the parents still need support of a very high order, but some have advanced to the stage where they no longer need to be in such close contact with the centre (although their children continue to use the day nursery), and only receive weekly or even fortnightly visits from the staff.

The NSPCC Battered Child Research Department feels that its success is largely due to the level of cooperation gradually developed with other agencies since the project began. As Ray Castle says, 'One of the largest stumbling blocks in this field is the barrier which different professionals often put up against producing a combined service. There's got to be tremendous cooperation and a multi-disciplinary approach with everyone recognizing everybody else's expertise, and this was the main thing that we had to build up here in the initial stages. Once you can get everybody looking towards the fact that they all want to achieve the same thing – the protection of the child and the prevention of an attack recurring – that's the point at which everyone suddenly realizes how much benefit there is in having a treatment service available.'

I will finish this section on the Department with the comment he made after we had been looking round the nursery one day where groups of healthy-looking children were happily occupied with their play : 'It sounds a terrible thing to say in the circumstances, but yes, I'm a happy man. Sometimes I despair at the size of the problem, but then I think of those kids in there – don't forget that many of them we first saw lying in hospital covered in tubes and bandages – and I feel better. Some of them would probably have been dead or crippled by now. But they're not. That thought's enough for me.'

Let us finish by reviewing quickly some of the other advances which are being made. Health Centres, which are being opened at an encouraging rate, provide preventative as well as curative medicine. Many include school health services, child health, antenatal care facilities, family planning services, physiotherapy, crèches, and above all a centre of contact between doctors, social workers, health visitors, psychiatrists, and anyone else working with a family. Where space for relaxation and community activities is provided as well, such a building can become a real community centre, and in such an atmosphere it should not be too difficult to recruit mothering aids and other helpers.

Another interesting scheme is the Family First Trust, which is now well established in Nottingham. Just as Oxfam prefers to give people tractors so that they can grow their own crops rather than spoonfeed them with ready-grown food, so Family First provides houses for the homeless and security for the lonely and deserted, so that they can look after themselves. Since it was founded in 1966 it has housed over 600 families, and now the trust is happy to report that it 'can begin to see the longer-term results of its early work. Many of the young women who came in need of urgent help discovered, often for the first time in their lives, that they were wanted and that they were able to help others whose circumstances were even worse. There is no clear line between those who need help and those who give it. Ruth Johns, Director of the Trust says : 'I agree with you that many people are at some time in a pre-battering state. I feel very strongly that most women need at least one or two older or similarly aged women close to them emotionally and in terms of physical distance (i.e. in the same road or street or round the corner) when their family is very young, especially while babies are very tiny. Even women whose husbands are loving and competent usually have this need.

'This Trust houses mainly unsupported mothers, many of

them very young. A significant number of the mothers have themselves had institutional upbringings or have unsatisfactory home backgrounds and no "roots". They need their own home and independence but also need to be within a community which accepts them and in which they find it easy to make close friends. A young insecure mother with a baby which cries all night needs to have someone whom she can talk to, to take the stress out of the situation.

'We find that the young mothers develop very high standards of mothering, and I can only attribute this to the fact that:

1 We do not allow past records about the young women to stop them being given the chance to prove they can cope independently.

2 They live within a very informal "community" which is self-helping and encourages initiative and confidence.

'*Institutionally reared girls who had babies in their mid-teens have turned out to be self-assured young women and very able mothers: it is not necessary for the problems of one generation to be transferred to the next.*'

Talking in general about battered babies, she continues: 'Many babies and small children are subjected to too harsh "punishment" by mothers who feel guilty, hopeless and tired. Mothers need loads of encouragement to express themselves as mothers in their own way and not be driven into guilty feelings by other people's ideas of what is "normal" and "right". Professional advisers are not always terribly helpful when it comes to building up confidence! Teachers, social workers, etc., can in fact sometimes add to a mother's feelings of insecurity rather than give her the confidence to do her job better.'

Yet another idea which is being experimented with is to impose enforced periods of community service as a 'punishment' for certain offences. In the few cases where this has been applied to mothers who have injured their own children it appears so far to have been successful. Obviously great care will have to be taken in choosing which parents can usefully be given this form of punishment – if punishment it must be called: an increase in feelings of guilt is going to help no one. But where such a parent is able to positively aid other families and feel herself or himself of genuine use, surely there will be an increase in confidence. Not all workers in this field would agree; they argue that the battering parent should not be expected to meet the community's needs and that what they require is exactly the opposite, for the community to support *them*. While this is true, it is also true that at present society as a whole demands some form of punishment for certain offences, and work which gives such a parent a chance to build up a sense of self-respect is certainly a great deal better than incarceration in prison. Observations of the results over a period of time must be studied, however, in order to prove which argument is right.

Sir Keith Joseph has popularized the phrase 'cycle of deprivation' and it will be very interesting to see what positive results are obtained from the actions he planned to take. Among social workers and others there is a general cynicism that not much more than words can be expected. However, the movement is in the right direction: if words are also accompanied by cash then perhaps the cycle may indeed stand a chance of being broken.

Meanwhile each tragedy which hits the headlines has some effect. The case mentioned earlier where a two-year-old child was killed a few weeks after having been returned to its parents resulted nine months later in an overhaul of the proceedings of the county involved. 'The social services committee says talks have taken place with hospital authorities to ensure the free flow of information between agencies dealing with battered babies and their families. Guidance to social workers has been revised and general practitioners, probation and child guidance services have been told of the revised procedure for notifying cases of suspected battering. The new procedures have also been closely defined in talks with the director of the NSPCC. The committee recommends the setting up of family advice centres to help families which are at "risk"' (*Guardian*). The Maria Colwell case is likely to be even more effective: let us hope there will not have to be many more victims before all the necessary action is taken.

These, then, are some of the ways in which progress is being made. The future is hopeful, and as the social services settle down after their reorganization the present problems should gradually be ironed out. The social worker is in the forefront of the battle to save children from being abused, and they need every scrap of help they can get from every possible source.

Chapter 6
The police

In an address to the Royal Society of Health in 1972 a doctor who has had more opportunity than most to study the subject, said, 'Few aspects in the management of these children generate such heat as the involvement of the police. . . The two positions are widely polarized; on the one hand there are the enthusiasts who maintain that under no circumstances whatsoever should the police ever become involved; at the other extreme there are police forces who insist that since the physical injury of a child is a crime, the concealment of these cases is unlawful, and all these injuries to children should be reported to them. Clearly this is an intolerable situation and the doctor, in the centre of two such clearly differing views, must give serious thought as to the attitude he must adopt in these circumstances.

'In general, the police in these situations receive the cooperation . . . they deserve. If a force is determined to prosecute irrespective of whether it be a deliberate assault or whether it be a battered baby, then they will receive very little cooperation. If on the other hand they are prepared to play their part in the management they can expect to receive the cooperation of the personnel engaged in dealing with the situations.'

Many policemen would deny that last sentence. They say that however willing they are, there are still many workers in the field – particularly social workers – who distrust them and will give them no information whatsoever unless the assault is so severe that there is no option. Most doctors may be won round more easily, but even there prejudice dies hard. It may be an unpalatable fact for many policemen but the truth is that if they are to receive any worthwile cooperation they have no choice but to agree not to prosecute except in severe cases where everyone agrees prosecution is necessary.

That there exist almost diametrically opposite views among

policemen is not particularly surprising – no one imagines every policeman to be identical – but the remarkable variability of action taken in different cases may surprise those who are not aware of the extent to which county police forces are autonomous. Each force is responsible to itself only: what the Chief Constable of Northampton decides to do on a particular issue may be identical to or the complete opposite of what his counterpart in Dorset does; the decisions are theirs alone, and unless they are clearly behaving in a bizarre or dishonest manner they will not be interfered with by the Home Office (beyond perhaps being given occasional advice). Nevertheless, in general there is probably less difference in certain basic attitudes among policemen than there is in most professions. There can be few, if any, policemen who do not believe absolutely in law and order and in the value of self-control. I can think of no other profession where you could take such a homogeneity of certain personality traits for granted.

It is this basic similarity in attitude among the police which occasionally wrecks the most well-meaning attempts of some of them to come to a working compromise with workers in other fields. Doctors and social workers on the whole learn to hide their personal reactions, putting their professional face forward. Policemen, who perhaps more than most have chosen their job as a result of their personal attitudes, seem less adept at keeping up a smooth line of talk without revealing sooner or later their own inner feelings with regard to the subject of law and order. So that a policeman genuinely wanting to help a battering mother may almost succeed in gaining the confidence of her social worker, but may then lose that trust completely by commenting that he can't help feeling that the woman could have stopped herself from attacking the child if she had really wanted to. At once the social worker puts him back into the category of 'punitive official' and sets about protecting his client from the spectre of the law.

In a previous chapter we looked at several complaints about social workers made by the police. Let us now see what social

workers and the medical profession have to say about policemen (bearing in mind these complaints come from areas where
a working pattern of cooperation between all of them has not
yet been established). From the Director of Social Services of a
large London borough : 'I don't think the police in fact have
much contribution to make in a society which gets anguished
not only about the injury to the child but also about the pres-
sures on the mother and father which led to that injury. I have
talked for hours with the police about the point at which we
should tell them we've discovered an injury to a child which
might be the result of a battering, but all they seem concerned
with is calling the mother into the station and saying, right,
this is a chargeable offence. Now that is a largely irrelevant act
as far as I am concerned. No, we don't go racing after the police
as soon as we hear of an injury because I think British law lives
just about a century behind the times. We don't really keep
them in the dark, but we try to steer the situation along in
such a way that the notion of a police enquiry is the last in the
line of a sequence of actions rather than the first.'

This comment was typical; even where I had spoken to
policemen and women in an area and knew for a fact that some
at least were highly sympathetic, amongst the social workers
concerned I would still often come across almost total distrust
and a refusal to risk cooperation. 'It's not like the police tell
you,' they insist. 'They'll bring a charge of attempted murder if
they've half a chance, and then everything you've done is
wrecked. Even if they don't do that, they *accuse*, and that's un-
bearable to these mothers.'

Psychiatrists, with the mental health of the patients upper-
most in their minds, can be even more outright. One London
psychiatrist said, 'The police are just acting as agents of vengeance, that's all, they're acting as society's super-ego conscience
to attack those who've done wrong : if you've bashed your child
then you must be bashed too. If there's a child with a severe
feeding problem, that's up to the paediatrician; the police never
get involved with a feeding problem, do they? Yet the emotional problems involved might be very similar indeed to that of

a battered baby. The police's job is to deal with anti-social disorders, and to view a mother–child problem as an anti-social disorder is obviously the wrong frame of reference. For the police to come along to investigate at this stage and decide whether they should make a charge is terrible. It's a time of potential tragedy for the family, and the police have absolutely no place in this at all. As it stands the law is quite adequate : if a child is in danger it can be taken into care without any need for police intervention.'

Hospitals, the greatest source of referrals to the NSPCC, rarely call in the police in the first instance. In a few rare areas the local social services insist on all cases being referred to the police regardless of how minor or unproven the attack – an in- stance was given in a previous chapter of a paediatrician, asking for a social worker to call on a stressed parent and two uni- formed policemen arriving instead. But such a policy seems to be unusual : normally quite the opposite is the case. As the same paediatrician pointed out : 'In medicine we are simply not prepared to make a diagnosis until we have all the signs and symptoms and tests in front of us. You can't come to a snap decision as to whether a child has been battered : it takes time to be certain, and it's pointless bringing in the police until you are sure. Even then I won't do it unless I think the child is going to have to be taken into care and it happens to come from one of the areas where it's necessary to get police cooperation for that.'

The psychiatrist's point about the police acting as our agents of vengeance is of course partly true. Few people can be so humane that they will wish no punishment to be meted out to parents who have killed or very severely maimed their children. A psychiatrist spends his day investigating the underlying reasons behind human action : when therefore he considers some terrible act a man or woman has done he looks at it as an end result and judges it accordingly, or, more likely, forbears to judge at all. But most people see such a crime as an isolated act and are not seriously concerned with its background : an old lady lies battered to death on the ground – beside that fact what does it matter that her assailant had a drunk father and an inadequate mother? A bank manager is shot dead and his young secretary blinded, her face scarred for life – who is interested that the murderer grew up in a slum and was self-conscious about his puny stature? Most of us demand punishment in these cases, and we employ the police to see that the criminal is caught. The police as a whole are unlikely ever to be fore-runners of reform; the public probably gets what it asks for, and if the most progressive radicals are frustrated in their desires for penal reform so, fortunately, are the die-hard conservatives who would bring back the birch and the scaffold.

A hospital doctor discussing his dislike of calling in the police, explained his own attitude with regard to extreme battering. 'Of course I've not been talking about the dangerously ill, severely damaged children. I think that, although in principle it's the same thing, any doctor would feel that in such a gross situation the community is going to demand that such a parent face criminal proceedings. I don't think it's logical, but it's ex-pedient. If a child is killed you can't say, we don't believe in punishing parents for this. It's murder, and – whatever the extenuating circumstances are – that is not for us to deal with. The police could say this is illogical, they could say a severely battered child is no different from a child failing to gain weight, because they're not being looked after properly. In principle that's absolutely right, but one's got to face up to the fact that one lives in a world of reality and expediency. I don't report somebody who parks on a yellow line but I do report somebody who breaks into a house. Somebody who has committed murder must suffer the punishments of the community.'

The decision to bring in the police is easy where a child is clearly dying. But sometimes a head injury might not appear very severe even to the examining doctors, and a child may suffer a relapse some months after the injury. In this case if they were not told of the injury when it happened the police may find it almost impossible to check up on facts. They argue that it may be in the parents' own interest for the police to investigate immediately. If a person dies within a year and a day as a result of an inflicted injury then a homicide charge will be brought against the person responsible under one of three headings: murder, manslaughter or infanticide. A mother suffering from postnatal depression who kills her child within twelve months of its birth will probably merely be put under probation, but the police may have only the social worker's word as to the mental state of the mother if they are brought into the case four or five months after the assault has taken place. By then the mother will probably be quite incoherent about what happened at the time of the attack and the police will feel dissatisfied with their investigations. The medical argument is that even if the police had seen the mother at the time the injury was sustained they would not in any case have been properly qualified to diagnose postnatal depression.

The doctors fear the effect on the parent and her relations with her child if the police enquiries are accusative: the police reply that they must know about assaults of any kind, it's their job to know. But as a psychiatrist pointed out, 'If the child is going to live there's absolutely no point in calling in the police, it only confuses matters and makes treatment more difficult. If the child dies, there still would have been no point. They would have been too late to protect the child, and if it's only public vengeance they're after, then they can get it after the child is dead. After all, if someone is being poisoned they don't expect the murderer to give them evidence while it's going on, do they? They have to do the best they can after the victim's dead. There's no difference that I can see.'

When I put the police's argument – that they are there to protect the child as much as the parent – to the paediatrician mentioned earlier, he replied, 'You can't do one without the other. Anyway, it's not true. The police's job is to detect crime and to put it to the court for the court's decision whether to punish or not to punish. *That's* the primary aim of the police, to detect crime, not to protect the child or to see that it's rehabilitated with its family – that's the job of the social workers and the doctors.'

To this the police will reply that very often the families need separating from each other, even if only temporarily while feelings cool down, and that only the police can be sure of succeeding in bringing a case successfully to the Juvenile Courts. Magistrates faced with a social worker who is not only uneasy in his mind about separating families even though he is actually asking the court for a care order, but who is also untrained in the finer aspects of court procedure, may well decide to go against that social worker's request and leave a child in the bosom of its family out of misplaced sentiment. Even if a care order is placed on an infant it can easily be rescinded by another court a few months later (without any systematic investigation into the background of the case being undertaken): many tragedies have happened as a result of children being returned to their families too soon. Police often prefer to bring cases to the Criminal Courts when they suspect a child is in danger of a really severe battering, as an appeal against a Criminal Court ruling is far less likely to succeed.

They might thus have achieved their fully justified aim of physical separation in a severe case, but the question still remains of what will happen when the child is eventually returned home. The parent's relationship with his child is hardly likely to have been improved by a successful convicion. On the other hand, the police might have been absolutely correct in their judgement; if the child had not been physically separated from its parents it would have already been dead and there would have been no relationship left to worry about.

The truth is it is almost impossible to know what action is correct in any particular case: only after a tragedy has occurred can we be certain who was right. The cases where gentler treatment was successful and nothing further happened do not make headlines. Occasionally a situation can be so clearly dangerous that no one has any doubt as to what action should be taken, but the prejudice against the police is so strong that even then they might not be called in until it is too late for them to find out exactly what did happen.

It is probably quite clear from the general tone of this book that I sympathize deeply with the parents, but I must admit that in some of the cases I have come across I feel that the police are justifiably annoyed that they were not called in earlier. Let me quote one example which comes from an area where the police forces are highly sympathetic to the problem of battering, and certainly do not prosecute unless they are certain it is necessary for everybody's sake. The colour slides they showed me were of a baby girl a few months old with gaping stab wounds around the pubic area at the top of the thighs, both front and back.

'That kid was brought into hospital on a Friday afternoon – the casualty officer knew they were knife marks, the consultant knew they were knife marks, but he thought he was doing the right thing in contacting the social services. Unfortunately they close down here on Friday evenings so nothing happened until Monday. They went to see the father (who'd done the stabbing) and got the usual sort of yarn from him about a fox terrier having bitten the baby. It was not until Tuesday that we heard about it, and even then it was by accident, so there was a four-day-old line to follow which had been fouled up by the previous investigations. Now in fact in that case we did bring a prosecution – there was never any choice. The whole family had been under the social services for some time – it was a real problem family, subnormal and incapable. The bloke who did the stabbing – he'd already got a record of violence – was not only the child's father, but the mother was his sister. It wasn't just casual between them – they lived together almost like man and wife in the same house as the rest of the family – and it was all right until the girl (she was only 15) took up with a proper boy friend. I suppose out of jealousy the brother suddenly stabbed the baby and damn nearly killed it. We had no choice but to get him away, and he's in the local mental hospital at the moment, diagnosed as a psychopath. God knows what else would have happened if he'd been left with his family, as he might have been if we hadn't stepped in.'

That particular event took place three or four years ago, and the police force involved think it unlikely that nowadays they would not be informed immediately if such a case were to happen again. But many areas have not yet achieved a successful rapport between the police and other services, and in these such a situation could still easily arise. It takes a great deal of experience to decide how dangerous a situation is and what sort of action must be taken immediately : whoever makes such a decision must be a senior person capable of looking at the available facts without prejudice.

The real difficulty lies less with the dramatic kind of case just discussed than with those where only mild injuries are involved. Often these are not even definitely recognized as having been inflicted by the parent : several doctors pointed out to me that they have been trained to accept the patient's word, and if his or her explanation sounds reasonable they do not go out of their way to look for trouble. Certainly there seems to be no reason for the police to be involved in mild cases on an active level, though in areas where they are fully cooperating and serve on consulting committees their local knowledge of certain problem families can be invaluable as a source of extra information. However, there are still many policemen and women who would not care to accept a passive role as dispensers of local knowledge, and these will continue to pay for their freedom to take action as they see fit, regardless of the desires of the other bodies involved, by only being informed of the most violent cases.

Perhaps the root of the dissension between the police and almost everybody else involved in the treatment of battering families lies in their differing attitudes to punishment. The situation is further complicated by the fact that many ordinary members of the public are ambivalent about the value of punishment : intellectually they may decide that punishment is ineffective as a treatment, but they themselves have been brought up to expect punishment to follow wrong-doing and they are uneasy with a situation where this does not happen.

The police are single-minded on the question of punishment. Although they insist their job is the detection of crime and that their prime interest is not punitive, it is unlikely that someone who doubted the virtues of punishment for wrongdoing would join the police force in the first instance, just as one would not expect a vegetarian to become apprenticed to a butcher.

It is instructive to see what various policemen and women, all of whom are interested in and sympathetically-minded about baby battering, have to say. The reader should bear in mind that they are speaking of their sincere beliefs, and are not merely handing out the official line which they have not considered and thought about. For those to whom such ideas about behaviour seem shocking in the light of today's popular psychology, I would suggest they try to understand the attitude behind the words, because it is probably the attitude of the majority of people in this country. What is best for a society may not necessarily be best for an individual, although this unpalatable fact is very difficult to accept in an individualistic society like our own.

'Battering parents expect to get punished, you must realize that. They've been brought up that if they've done wrong they'll get whacked for it, and if they don't then they feel society is saying, it's all right, we don't mind what you've done. Then they go and do it again.' From another area, 'Why shouldn't someone who's broken one of society's rules be punished? What's wrong with punishment? As long as it goes hand in hand with treatment, and when the punishment is over the crime is put away and forgotten. I know that's easier said than done, but it's not the concept of punishment that's at fault, it's society's treatment of the prisoner and his aftercare that's wrong. No, punishment is necessary in a well-run society, but punishment shouldn't mean shutting someone up in a cell without any treatment, then kicking them around afterwards when they come out.'

Many see the threat of punishment as an important part of prevention. 'Part of the value of a probation order is that if once you've been investigated by the police you know if you do it again the chances that you'll get away with only a probation order next time aren't so good. So you watch your step.' Similarly, 'The object of the exercise is the protection of the child.

To achieve that you may need to keep some form of sanction hanging over the parents' head to keep them on the straight and narrow. There's nothing wrong with that, you know. It's the theory of a little bit of healthy fear being good for you. Take me. I've got a nice job here, and I do it as well as I can, mostly because I like doing it but also because I'm frightened of what would happen if I didn't. At the back of my mind there's that little prod that keeps me going, and I see nothing wrong with it. With problem families you give all the help you can, but you have to watch they don't become so dependent on social services' help that they can't do anything for themselves. They need that little prod to keep them up to the mark, to stiffen them up, and to my mind that's a thoroughly good thing.' On guilt: 'They end up after psychiatric treatment being able to explain away their battering in psychiatric terms. They learn, you see, they learn how to talk quite glibly about all their childhood problems and they try to justify what they've done *instead of feeling guilt!* All right, so the psychiatrist says guilt is a bad thing, but *why* is it? There may be all sorts of reasons why she's done it, but it's a dreadful thing to do and she ought to realize that. I can't see why psychiatric treatment can't do two things, first make a mother aware of a sense of guilt about what she's done but, having felt that guilt, teach her to understand why it's happened so she can try not to let it happen again.'

A psychiatrist answers, 'It's true that if the parents are imprisoned or punished they often do feel better about what they've done – they feel they've paid for their crime – but I still don't see this as an adequate reason for bringing in the police. Society says you have to be punished and they accept it, it fits in with what they may want unconsciously, but that still doesn't make it the right course of action.'

Who then is right? The point of discussion is far wider than the narrow issue of baby battering. The whole world is going through a period of changing values, and as a nation we hardly know what we think on many issues. Although we may pay lip-service to the idea that a sense of guilt is bad for us, isn't guilt or something very like it the main weapon we still use to bring up our children with? Do that, and mummy'll be cross. Wrap up the message how you will, but basically a small child has somehow to be inhibited from carrying out many of his own natural wishes, both for his sake and for the sake of others. Later many other factors will motivate him, such as pride, a sense of achievement, a desire to help others, but at first it is probably something very like the policeman's 'sense of healthy fear' that teaches a child not to put his fingers in the electric socket, not to lick the icing off the cakes his mother has just put out on the table, not to knock his sister down the stairs because she won't let him play with her toy.

It is argued that battering parents have an over-developed sense of guilt, that they sometimes have a positively unhealthy desire to be punished which should not be indulged. All this is probably true, but the only fact which is quite clear is that the sense of indecision about moral values and about modes of behaviour in general which is currently endemic in British life, is making the treatment of these battering parents a subject of partisan guesswork. Until sufficient research is done it is impossible to know who in the long run is right about the value of inflicting guilt. When one meets these parents and gets to know them, it seems pointless to consider doing anything other than attempt to help them. But perhaps the police are right in feeling that, where there are no clear pointers to the way one should behave, many people will find it difficult to impose self-discipline on themselves, and as a result will grow lax and behave badly. Some therapeutic communities are managing to help disturbed people combine self-discovery with self-discipline, and this seems to be the most desirable aim to treatment.

Meanwhile the undoubted dangers of police intervention are summed up by Joan Court: 'Prosecution, if successful, is unlikely to have a deterrent effect on parents who are not capable of controlling their conduct, and merely confirms them in their negative self-image. If they are acquitted then they feel vindicated and justified in their conduct, and future therapeutic work with them may prove impossible. Most important of all, perhaps, is that the resultant publicity prevents other parents from seeking help in the early stages. The injured child, who could have been adequately protected through the Juvenile Court, is then in great danger.' Kempe adds a further thought: 'I view child abuse the way I view failed suicides, with much compassion. We no longer punish people who fail at suicide. Well, I think attacks on small children by their parents by and large are attacks on themselves and I would treat it in exactly the same fashion. Not as a police matter, but as a disease. After all, we've shown that punishing does not work. Gaol does not make you love more. In our experience there have been six parents who have gone to gaol; three have re-bashed their children, one has not, and two we've lost track of. So three out of four have failed to be reformed in prison. Prison, to these people, is simply reinforcement of what they have always known : that it's a punishing world and you deserve to be punished, so they think it's perfectly all right for society to punish them.'

When I talked to Chief Superintendent Wedlake of Scotland Yard, whose chief concern is the welfare of children in the Metropolitan area, she said she was well aware of all these arguments, and she confirmed that the police rarely hear about batterings from social workers and hospitals. Like every other policeman I met she felt this was unfair, a result of prejudice. 'One argument is always being used, that the police are a punitive organization, which we're *not*: we're merely a law-enforcing agency. It's quite wrong to say that because somebody goes before a court they are automatically punished. If they need help they will get it, and there'll be the power of the law behind them to make sure they not only have that help but that they take advantage of it. They very rarely go to prison, you know – they might get put on probation with the condition they have six months' residence and treatment at a mental hospital, for instance. It's often the only way to see that they do get treatment: if you just say – what about coming into hospital for a few weeks, it'll do you good – you won't get any-where, they'll refuse to come. And even if no action at all is taken against them in the end, it's not true to say they feel vindicated. There's a subtle way of saying – all right, we know perfectly well what's happened; nothing's being done this time, but if any harm comes to the child in future then action will be taken. And it works. They take much more notice than when a psychiatrist or a social worker hints at the same thing.'

All this may be true, but the fact remains that as long as baby battering comes under the Offences Against the Person Act (grievous bodily harm) it is a CID matter and in cases of serious injury an ordinary CID officer has no choice but to arrest and charge a parent. The only way out of this is for a high-ranking officer to be involved who is willing to take upon himself the responsibility of delaying police action while all the people involved including the police conduct their investigations and decide on the best way to treat the case. Even this method is denied by some forces, who insist that no one, however high-ranking, has any choice but to make an arrest in such an instance. One police force which does not take this viewpoint is the Northamptonshire Police.

The Northampton scheme evolved through a process of trial and error, the result of friendly cooperation between doctors, the CID and the local NSPCC officer. By 1971 the scheme was working sufficiently well for one of the originators of the scheme, Dr H. de la Haye Davies, Northampton's principal police surgeon, to write a report on it which was published in the *Police Journal*, presumably being seen by most police forces in the country. The scheme is now well-established and has the full support of most local doctors, though even in this area it is still rare for social workers to report cases direct to the police. As far as is known nothing else quite like it existed when the scheme was first launched, though no doubt by now other areas are working in a similar way. Because it has successfully overcome most of the hostility between the police and the other professions involved, I feel it is well worth setting out in some detail just how the scheme works.

The basic team consists of a consultant paediatrician, a senior police surgeon, a senior CID officer and a senior inspector of the NSPCC. It is of great importance in the formation of these teams that all the different professions are represented by senior men and women, as only someone of high rank can risk taking responsibility for the kind of decisions which occasionally have to be made. This is particularly important in the case of the police representative, who, when he reports back to his Chief Constable, will naturally find his judgement more highly valued, and more likely to be acted upon, if he is a senior; normally in Northampton either the Detective Superintendent or the Assistant Chief Constable is the officer involved. Members of the team contact each other informally, in the early stages great care being taken to see that nothing is committed to paper which might set in train certain actions which no one wants to take. Without mutual trust such a course would not be possible, and it says much for the tact of the main intermediary, in this case Dr Davies, and the willingness of Detective Superintendent Roy (the police officer most frequently involved) that the team has remained successfully viable for so long.

The team consider the consultant paediatrician to be the mainstay of the scheme. He must be prepared to admit a child at a moment's notice to one of his beds, to treat him until he is cured and then, when he has finally been returned home, to keep in touch with him through out-patient clinics and also through continued contact with the family doctor and the local social services.

The police surgeon, the second member of the team, is the liaison man between the medical profession and the law. He is in the advantageous position of having a foot in both camps and is able to appreciate both viewpoints. Within twenty-four hours of the child being admitted to hospital he will have seen and discussed the case with the consultant paediatrician, his forensic expertise being particularly useful in cases which are difficult to diagnose. Dr Davies gave as an example a baby he once examined, which at first was thought to have been battered. 'The mother found the child dead in its cot, but for some reason didn't report it for about three hours. There were several other suspicious factors as well: for one thing, we knew the mother was under psychiatric treatment. When the ambulance drivers brought it in they commented that there was some bruising round the penis and in one or two other places; it all seemed real text-book stuff, so I was whistled up quickly. But when I removed the kid's nappy I saw its stool was absolutely fluid. The bruising in fact was very early post-mortem degeneration, a skin change which is a perfectly natural thing and which had come on quickly because of virulent gastro-enteritis. I asked the pathologist to do a post-mortem straight away and it turned out that in addition to the rest it had the most virulent middle ear infection I've ever seen – both middle ear cavities filled with pus. Now if a doctor who wasn't expert in forensic science had looked at that child he might easily have interpreted it as a case of battering, and a lot of upset might have occurred before the real truth was discovered.'

One advantage of having a police surgeon examine an injured child is that it avoids the problems the paediatrician will otherwise face in attempting to build a good relationship with the child's parents at the same time as investigations are going on. Not only is the paediatrician relieved from having to deal directly with the investigating police other than through informal channels, but the principle of confidentiality between him and his patient, always a tricky problem in cases like this, is preserved. Further, if the case is taken to court, it is the police surgeon who will take on the task of presenting the medical evidence; were their own doctor to stand up and list in gruesome detail their child's injuries the parents would be likely to consider this a betrayal, whereas since they have no personal contact with the police surgeon they will merely regard him as an instrument of the law.

Another important point is that police surgeons, many of whom hold a Diploma of Medical Jurisprudence, have learned how to present a case properly and to stand by their opinion successfully against searching cross-examination. If a child is in danger and needs, however temporarily, to be separated from its parents, a successful outcome is essential. Clever lawyers can sometimes make mincemeat of men and women who are normally more than capable of holding their own, with the result that a number of children are returned to their families in spite of the expressed fears of the doctors or social workers who have been looking after them. Obviously this is less likely to happen when an experienced police surgeon is presenting the evidence. If a Care Order is being asked for and this is granted, then the child will be placed in the care of the local Social Services Department, and it will be the police surgeon who earns the opprobrium of the family for this action, rather than the paediatrician. It seems hard on the police surgeon that this should be so, but as Dr Davies says, 'My back's broad; what matters to me is the future welfare of the family, not who gets their gratitude.'

The third member of the team must be a senior police officer, and since battering is considered a criminal assault it will normally be the CID who will perform this function. As Dr Davies writes in his report, a CID officer with definite proof that someone has assaulted a child must 'put the evidence before those responsible for deciding whether a prosecution should be instituted, but in our experience, the latter person or persons invariably follow a human and proper course, and if it is in the best interests of the child that a prosecution should be avoided, then this line is usually taken'. Behind these official phrases lies the fact that the Chief Constable does in fact listen and listen hard. There have only been one or two instances of disagreement where police action was taken against the wishes of some of the other members of the committee, and they claim that much was learned from this.

The team, whose primary job is to collate all the information gathered by its various members and then decide the best course of action to be taken for the child and its family, is called together as soon as possible after the injury. The meetings are best kept informal : obviously the scheme would cease to work if each member went to the meeting grimly determined to wrest as much as possible from 'the other side'. In addition to the three previously mentioned members there will also be a NSPCC officer if he has been involved; any policeman or woman who has been working on the case – this might be a chief inspector or a sergeant; the social worker for the area, and the family's GP if he wants to come, though most decide not to. When the case has been talked about and looked at from every point of view a decision is arrived at, and this will be communicated back to police headquarters. From then on, every case is different, but whatever the final outcome, the team keeps in touch, informally by phone or by occasional meetings.

In a comparatively small county like Northampton it is difficult to produce sufficient statistical evidence to prove how successful or otherwise a scheme has been. Those involved in it can only say they have no doubts about its success and as the years go by they are more than ever convinced that such co-operation is vital in the treatment of battering families. Certainly the police there seem to be far more satisfied with the information they receive from their medical colleagues than others I met in less cooperative areas. Since the rate of battering does not seem to have gone up as a result of police lenience, perhaps other areas might be encouraged to follow suit.

In 1970 the Home Office sent out a directive to all Medical Officers of Health and Chief Constables, asking for meetings of social workers, police and doctors in which questions of co-operation could be discussed. By all accounts some of these meetings were not very successful. As one doctor put it, 'The social workers sat on one side of the hall, the police on the other, and we doctors sat in the middle between them. It was like throwing the fox to the hounds – they yapped at each other over our heads and neither side was prepared to give an inch. Whenever we opened our mouths it seemed to set off one side or the other, so in the end we just shut up and let them get on with it.'

The Home Office soon became aware of the poor cooperation between the police and the rest. A 1972 circular of theirs stated, 'The Department of Health and Social Security hopes that [this] report will stimulate further thought on the importance of co-operation between all the professionals involved and they have been careful to focus attention on the problem of refining the role of the police and on the police concern to be involved at the earliest possible moment.' But many feel that it is up to the Home Office to do something more positive than merely quote the hopeful sentiments of the Department of Health. I heard complaints that the Home Office does not give any clear guidance on this tricky problem, especially from doctors who say that quite often individual police officers admit they would prefer not to prosecute but that they have no choice in the matter. No doubt some officers hide behind this excuse and are in fact perfectly content to bring a prosecution, but there are certainly many others who would like not to but feel they dare not take a risk.

The same thing applies to police representation on hospital case committees: several doctors told me they have assured the local police they would welcome them provided they would agree to take no action except in severe cases, but nearly always the police reply that they would like to come but if they heard of anything they thought might be a crime, however confidentially they were told it, they would have to investigate – with the consequence that they are rarely asked on to these committees.

The same circular states: 'A battered baby case is by definition one in which there is at least a suspicion that a serious offence has been committed. *When a case comes to the notice of the police they are bound to investigate it* although a prosecution will not necessarily follow. Once the facts are known to them the police have to decide whether to prosecute . . .' [my italics]. On the other hand they admit: 'Police representation at the case committee level is reported in very few areas and this is a reflection of a reluctance of doctors and social workers to involve the police before they have been able to assess the social consequence of such action in situations which are so often complex.' But instead of drawing the obvious conclusion from these two facts, they finish up with a first-rate piece of officialese saying precisely nothing: 'This is one important area where greater flexibility may be needed and where attention should be focused on the possibility of improving cooperation between the police, doctors, nurses and social workers. It would be wrong to assume that the measure of cooperation necessary can be easily achieved but the encouragement of a continuing dialogue between all those concerned might hold out the best hope for the future.'

If a policeman sincerely believes he has no choice but to investigate and possibly prosecute on hearing of certain events, then the first statement above will reassure him he is correct in his belief. The last paragraph will in no way encourage him to cooperate since the first paragraph has just told him he must not. Let us be quite clear about this : to everybody except the police, police investigation at any level is not 'cooperation' unless it has been requested. Thus the second paragraph – 'police representation at the case committee level is reported in very few areas' – will continue to be true until the Home Office does something far more concrete than issue a few woolly statements to the effect they expect that it will probably all work out in the end. The Home Office is the only body who can make it work out, and they can only do so by issuing unequivocal directives which everybody can clearly understand. For example, where a paediatrician suspects a battering but does not consider the child's life to be at present endangered then the police should be informed so that they may know what is happening. The police in their turn should undertake to keep right out of the picture as far as the parents are concerned until a case committee (on which they would be represented) has decided what action ought to be taken. Where a case committee cannot come to an agreement then the argument will have to be taken to a further high-level committee, on which all professionals are represented, for arbitration. If, as at present, a doctor knows that the final decision will be made by a policeman, then he will not pass on information, and however many pious hopes the Home Office may express in future circulars, they will be doomed to remain unfulfilled.

It would be unfair to the Home Office, however, to leave the impression that its influence has been entirely negative. The various communications sent out over the past few years have certainly brought the existence of baby battering to the attention of many who might otherwise have preferred to ignore it. The first action was taken in 1970 when the Home Office asked for inter-professional discussions on a local basis.

In a memorandum entitled *The Battered Baby* (February 1970) the syndrome was described in some detail. It was a fair summing-up owing much to the NSPCC's research, though its tone was not always that used by the NSPCC's Research Department (for example, hospital casualty officers are instructed when talking to battering parents that, throughout, the parents must be told repeatedly that the first concern of the doctor is to make their child better and secondly, 'to make sure that it does not happen again.'). In May 1972 they sent out the circular quoted on page 140 which was the analysis of all the reports submitted to them as a result of the consultations they had requested in 1970.

This 1972 report was a broad-based review of what was being done all over the country, and contained various suggestions for improvement. From the analysis it appears that in the majority of counties police were included in the review committees, but these were merely general committees which were supposed to discuss what could be done locally to deal with baby battering in principle; although some meetings no doubt proved valuable, others resulted in the kind of polite squabble described a few pages back. The Home Office analysis suggests that these committees should meet regularly, and that their function should be to 'ensure that research, education and training programmes are carried out', also that they should cooperate with review committees in other areas to 'ensure that management procedures are either uniform or the differences clearly known and understood'. These are sound ideas, but not a great deal seems to have happened as a result, whether through local lethargy, a lack of funds or a lack of time it is difficult to judge.

The second type of committee which local authorities were encouraged to set up was the case committee, designed to deal with individual cases; basically this works on the Northampton pattern, where the police cooperate wholeheartedly. Unfortunately, the Home Office analysis proved that in most areas the police are very rarely invited to these case committees, for the reasons already explained. Again and again in the report the importance of what we might call the three 'c's' is stressed – coordination, communication and cooperation. But pious hopes are not enough : the Home Office knows what needs to be done – they themselves have made it clear in their own circular – so when will they accept that progress on the vexed question of police cooperation must originate from them? It is one of Britain's strengths as a nation that on the whole our police are incorruptible and that they follow the rules they are given. We do not want a police force that can change or adapt the rules as they see fit : the dangers are too great. Therefore it is essential they are given a clear lead where issues such as baby battering confuse the normal process of the law.

Not all policemen will agree with the concept of special rules for baby batterers, and some will object strongly. As one policewoman pointed out to me, 'Many of the policemen on the beat are young fathers and when they see what some man has done to his poor bloody kid their first instinct is to take their jackets off and have a go. It needs a tremendous amount of self-restraint on their part, you know, to keep control under those circumstances.' Nevertheless all policemen dislike the public image they have gained in recent years and feel they are not given sufficient credit for the large amount of social work they do as part of their job. The role of the policeman in society needs to be perpetually re-examined. In an age of mass communication some of the approbrium attached to police in less tolerant societies than ours has brushed off on to our own far milder police : if they are to restore the image of the friendly neighbourhood policeman (and that is how most of those I have talked to seem in essence to see themselves) then they must do more than make protesting noises when they are attacked. They will have to be seen making positive gestures of goodwill as a body, even if it involves them in some sacrifice of their own indepedence. After all, no one in the public services is any longer acting as a solitary unit. Modern social welfare is part of such a complicated structure that it can only function success- fully if the interests of the people who are being helped are put before departmental ambitions. The police are no exception and should not be treated as such unless they wish to remain quite apart from other professions and be seen purely as a detecting, punitive force. The choice has to be made, and the sooner it is made the better.

Chapter 7

The medical point of view

Criticisms of the police and the social services have been examined in earlier chapters, but there is one important professional body which rarely comes under attack : the medical profession. At present many aspects of medical training are inadequate and wrongly centred. If, for example, doctors were trained to treat patients as part of a family unit the incidence of battering could drop dramatically. Almost as important is the fact that medical students are not taught about healthy bodies, healthy families; the emphasis is not on maintaining health but on repairing damage. They learn about different parts of the body, are taught what can go wrong with these separate bits, and what they can do to put them right again. They learn about *sick* people, and they are taught to be interested in illness, not in achieving health, just as until recently nearly all psychiatry was founded on the study of mentally sick people, deductions from these studies then being popularly applied to healthy people as though there were no difference between them and the mentally sick.

The result of this wrongly-biased training is that to most young casualty officers in hospital emergency wards a man coming in with a broken leg is literally a 'broken leg'. The remainder of the man scarcely exists for the doctor – the body which the leg normally supports, the head controlling the body, is of little interest, and the home the man comes from, his marital relations, his success or failure in his job, none of these matter in the slightest. Now where an accidentally broken leg is concerned, these details are not especially relevant (though even here recovery may be delayed if the man is worried about losing his job or keeping up his hire-purchase repayments), but if it is an ulcer the man is suffering from, or if the patient is a child with a fractured arm or a burned hand, then it is of the utmost importance that the examining doctor should have been taught something about people as members of a family unit rather than people as individual collections of different limbs and organs.

Unfortunately such training is rare. Some teaching hospitals do now try to include a lecture on the subject and another lecture or two on problems particular to children, but not every student attends every lecture. Since an understanding of the patient within his family setting is not yet demanded of the qualifying student, a hangover, a heavy cold, or a piece of work waiting to be finished can tempt a young student to skip what does not seem to him to be a lecture of particular importance.

When, therefore, a year or so later, the brand-new casualty officer is faced with a small baby with a nasty bruise and a cut on his head he willingly believes the mother's explanation that the previous day she had walked too quickly through a door while carrying the baby, catching its head on the door jamb. No one has taught him to be suspicious of the twenty-four hours' delay in reporting the accident, typical in cases of battering, no one has warned him that such mothers can be very convincing liars; not even bothering therefore to wonder how the rather peculiarly shaped cut could possibly have been caused under such circumstances, he tells the nurse to slap a plaster over the cut, and sends the woman back home together with her baby. After all, she is obviously devoted to it and is furious with herself for having been so careless. It would have been insulting to have undressed the baby to see if there were any other bruises, even if he had thought of it (which to be honest he didn't, just as he did not think to have the baby weighed to see if it was an appropriate weight for its age). As there is no compulsory registration of suspected battering cases there would have been little point in his trying to find out quickly if the baby had been seen at any other local hospitals, and he was too busy to check in the normal way. He could not know, therefore, that twice in the last three months the mother had taken her baby to another hospital, once with a similar head wound and once with a fractured leg.

Our young doctor is not stupid; on the contrary, he is an intelligent ambitious young man. His present aim is to emulate as closely as possible the chief paediatrician of his hospital, a very impressive man whom he deeply admires. The paediatrician himself would not have found that particular small baby any more interesting than did his young casualty officer : now had it been in the same class as yesterday's newly-born spina bifida case or the hole-in-the-heart baby the consultant was examining at the very moment the plaster was being stuck on the doomed baby's head, it would have been another matter. Many hours and much money will be spent on the spina bifida baby who will die anyway at six months old, but the basically sound little battered baby will not live even as long as that unless somebody realizes very quickly what is happening.

The myth that doctors are omniscient creatures whose wisdom is above reproach dies hard. General practitioners, whose egos are not bolstered by daily contact with an obsequious staff, have far more opportunity to attain a proper understanding of the limits of their own capabilities, and a good GP is one of the most valued members of the community. But hospital consultants are encouraged to remain remote, almost divine, creatures. I still remember the disbelief with which I watched (indeed was forced to take part in) the fuss which took place when the chief gynaecologist did his rounds in the maternity ward in which I was lying. Encircling students fawned on him, nurses hovered, and there was even an anxious placatory smile on the face of the sister, normally a goddess in her own right. It was like partaking in some ancient regal ceremony : I doubt if even the Queen has quite as much servile attention paid to her as that lavished on some top consultants.

Fortunately for the progress of medicine there are many men and women of a quite different calibre, and in such hospitals a different atmosphere rules. However, even where the chief paediatrician himself is concerned with the problem of battered babies, it is not always easy for him to ensure that every possibly suspect case arriving at the emergency room is reported to him. There is still a great resistance among doctors just as there is amongst the general public to the fact of battering, and it will take a fair amount of persuasion on the part of the pae-diatrician before he can convince some of his juniors that it is a less rare phenomenon than they would like to suppose.

Nurses also have difficulty in coping with their reactions to baby battering. There exist training courses on children's ill-nesses in which the need to treat a child as part of a family unit is taught, but not all nurses elect to take this extra train-ing. Since any nurse may be called upon to look after a battered child, even if only temporarily until it can be placed in a special children's ward, it would seem advisable that all nurses be given some training in the subject. A shocked accusing nurse could cause a parent to remove the child arbitrarily from hospital care, with possibly disastrous results, but how could a young eighteen-year-old girl with no understanding of the stresses upon that parent be expected to behave otherwise as she gazes down at some poor little bruised infant lying mute in its cot, knowing that the man or woman standing beside her actually attacked it?

There is no system of compulsory refresher courses for either doctors or nurses, so that theoretically it is possible for half a century to pass before everyone concerned in medical care is taught about child abuse, even if such teaching were to start tomorrow. Such pamphlets as those issued by the Ministry of Health may be circulated among all members of staff in some of the more conscientious hospitals, but even then it is up to individual members as to whether or not they bother to read them. As for GPs, if they choose to avoid the subject it is only too easy for them to do so. Certainly the social services receive very few references from GPs of suspected baby battering cases, and yet most, if not all, battering parents and their children will have been seen, sometimes repeatedly, by their family doctors. Occasionally evidence of battering is simply not forthcoming, but sometimes after a child has died various facts emerge which prove highly embarrassing to a doctor who did not draw the right conclusion from a variety of factors which to another more experienced man would have clearly pointed to a diagnosis of battering. One such case, where everybody concerned – social workers, the NSPCC, doctors – were given warning after warning and yet nothing was done to save the child, will be detailed in the final chapter. The only way to prevent the recurrence of such a terrible mistake is for an intensive period of training to be made mandatory for everyone in the field, and that includes all already-qualified doctors and nurses, however old or experienced in general medical matters they may be.

It might be argued that interest in baby battering has suddenly become so widespread, with severe cases receiving such wide press coverage, that it ought to be impossible for any doctor to remain unaware of the syndrome. Yet some doctors still deny that baby battering, as distinct from other forms of child abuse, even exists. This myopia may be partly caused by the fact that some doctors are impatient of anything that smacks of psychiatry, preferring a nice batch of bacteria you can examine under a microscope. Several times I heard the phrase used about keenly interested doctors, 'Oh, they've got battered babies on the brain, they see them everywhere'.

The popular psychiatric explanation of the common refusal to recognize a battered child is that many people cannot face up to the violence in themselves, but it must also be borne in mind that a doctor has inbuilt inhibitions against suspecting his patients. His training has taught him that people expect to come to him in confidence with their illnesses, trusting that he will cure them, and that parents with sick children bring them to him in a similar spirit. That the child's illness may have been caused by the very mother who has come to him voluntarily and who is now so anxiously holding out her child is foreign to all he has been taught. He simply does not expect to find that a mother has injured her own child and therefore does not look for signs of abuse.

Dr James Cameron has clearly stated the medical attitude: 'On being presented with a child who shows signs of bruising, subdural haematoma and one or more fractured bones, a doctor, because of his training, will first tend to be concerned with the nature and extent of the injuries rather than their cause, possibly looking for some unusual syndrome, perhaps of genetic origin, to account for the condition. Secondly, unless he has obvious grounds for doing otherwise, he will be inclined to accept the history, whatever the discrepancy with his findings, at its face value. The thought that an adult in a position of trust could be responsible for the child's condition is so repugnant to natural feeling that it does not come to mind.'

A paediatrician comments: 'I'm afraid your outlook has to be the complete antithesis of a normal medical approach and for a doctor this is very, very disturbing. You mustn't believe what the patient is saying, yet at the same time you have to help them and above all take steps to protect the child. It's a very great strain.'

The question of confidentiality has caused much heart-searching among doctors. Doctors may not divulge information given to them by their patients unless those patients have given them permission to do so. Where a parent has admitted to battering but refuses to allow the doctor to pass on what he has told him, then the doctor, if he is going to obey strict medical ethics, has no choice but to remain silent. However, such a course is clearly impossible if a child's life appears to be endangered. This problem is being considered by the various medical bodies concerned, and no doubt some guidance will be laid down for future conduct, but for the present many doctors have to find their own way out of this problem. If the parents can be persuaded to talk to a social worker the doctor's ethical problems are over, as social workers are not similarly bound to silence.

A further complication for doctors who understand something of the mentality of battering parents and yet consider themselves bound by the code of professional ethics, is that they will realize that these parents are coming to them with an unspoken plea to be stopped from hurting their children. Few doctors are capable of solving such a problem on their own without the specialized help of supportive agencies, but if the parent insists on secrecy the doctor is not supposed to ask for such help! It is small wonder that many doctors prefer to turn a blind eye to the whole situation, especially when you consider that, in addition to the problem of confidentiality, if in the end the case finishes up in court the doctor may well be called on to give evidence, which he will find both time-consuming and distressing.

Baby battering is not like measles: it has been estimated that the average doctor may not see more than three or four cases in his working life, which will not allow him to grow very expert at recognizing the disease. This may well turn out to be a conservative estimate, however; in the two very different cities of New York and Denver between 250 to 300 cases are being reported per million population each year. If these figures hold true for Britain, and there seems to be no reason why they should not, we might expect something like two and a half thousand cases to be reported every year in Greater London alone. If this number seems unexpectedly high it should be considered that in 1968 New York had fewer than 800 cases reported (they already had a much higher reporting rate than Britain owing to the interest inspired by Kempe's early work and the fact that reporting is mandatory anyway), which leapt to 1,700 in 1969 and over 2,700 in 1970, a steep increase in only three years. This reporting rate is seen not as a rise in the incidence of battering but as a greatly increased recognition rate.

A similar increase in reported cases could occur in England in the near future, particularly if the reporting of all suspected cases were to become mandatory here too. In 1972 Dr M. Hall, after studying the incidence of battering cases brought to his Emergency and Accident Department in Preston, estimated that between five and six hundred children might be expected to die each year in Britain from battering. Yet the 1970 Home Office report showed that for 1967 (incredible as it may seem, there are no more recent figures available) a total of only seventy-one deaths of children under the age of five which were found to be due to 'homicide and injury purposely inflicted by other persons', forty-three of which deaths occurred in the first year of life. Since Dr Hall's estimate is likely to prove too small rather than too high – some people put the figure as high as 700 – it will be realized how many deaths are occurring at the moment without anyone recognizing their true cause.

Most doctors are working to full capacity: how then can they be expected to spare time to investigate possible cases of battering and, as important, pre-battering? By pre-battering I mean a situation where children are chastized heavily but not yet to the point of assault, and where family stress is such that if it were suddenly increased at any time an attack might be made. A doctor may wonder about the origin of one or two bruises, and, knowing the family background, suspect that the bruises are not accidental. The best method is for him to call for experienced help immediately, but whether he is able to do so depends on many factors. Large numbers of doctors now work in a group practice, and some of these have been able to arrange that one or more local health visitors should visit the surgery once or twice a week to discuss with the doctors any social problems about which they are concerned. Old people suspected of under-nourishment, 'work-shy' men pleading non-existent illness, or a low-IQ housewife's inability to cope with household management, all these can be investigated by a tactful health visitor. Easiest of all from the entry point of view is a situation where an infant is in the house, as the visit will then look like a normal routine checking-up on any problems of feeding or general care. An experienced worker, bearing in mind the doctor's suspicions, should during this visit be able to sense any difficulties, and through repeated calls might well forestall any drastic developments.

Since success means that nothing has happened, there can obviously be no statistics to prove the value of this method, but a panel of doctors who described their own scheme to me told me that there were several children whom they considered were in danger who had received this attention, and not one has subsequently received any injuries. It is possible, of course, that in the families concerned there had been no particularly stressful incidents to tip the balance between the precarious state of pre-battering and battering, and that no attack would have taken place even without the intervention of the health visitors. Nevertheless, if only one out of a hundred children were actually saved from a battering by such a system, is that not well worth doing? And, hardly less important, the mental well-being of the other ninety-nine families may have been greatly improved by the considerate help they will have received. One can feel certain that if such action were taken over the entire country a significant decrease in battering would result.

The main obstacle to such progress is that the very areas most in need of such help are the least likely to get it. In poor districts general practitioners are likely to be overloaded and overworked while the health visitors are probably so busy they have little time to spare for routine visits to doctors' surgeries. Battering parents can be very convincing, and it takes a perspicacious doctor even to have a hunch that something might be wrong: if they do not have the willing follow-up support of their local welfare services it will not be feasible for the great majority of doctors to do anything other than hope for the best and ring for the next patient, even where they strongly suspect that all is not well.

For many parents the inevitable sequel to an unattended 'cry for help' will be a visit to a hospital, bearing a child with fractured limbs or skull. In such a case the casualty officer needs to be highly suspicious. Very few normally-cared-for young babies suffer such injuries. A father of three grown children once remarked to me when I was a brand-new mother and still very cautious about handling my seemingly fragile infant, 'You can drop a baby on the floor and maybe you'll dent the floor but you won't hurt the baby.' Exaggeration, of course, but nevertheless it does take a fair amount of force to break a child's young limbs, and any such injury ought to be investigated very carefully.

Friedman and Holter found in a recent American survey that the type of injury a child suffered had considerable significance. 156 children presented to the emergency room of a hospital were carefully checked, and 10 per cent were judged to have suffered physical abuse. Of the total 156 children, nearly 45 per cent suffered from lacerations, and over 20 per cent had swallowed some dangerous substance. About 12 per cent suffered head injuries, while figures for burns, fractures and other limb injuries were between 8 and 5 per cent each. Of those who were suspected of having been physically abused, however, only one child had suffered lacerations: all the rest fell into the small group with head injuries, burns, fractures and dislocations, abrasions and bruises. The inference was therefore made that children with lacerations and ingestions may be regarded as being unlikely to have been battered, but that those with the other types of injury should be examined with particular care. This differentiation in the type of injury may be explained by the fact that most attacks are thought to occur while the parent is physically caring for the child; a knife or some other instrument which could cause laceration is unlikely to be in the parent's hand at such a time; and so any injuries would be of the kind caused by direct physical contact. The figures involved in this survey are statistically small, but further research may well prove them to be valid, in which case they will be a useful guide to casualty officers trying to make a snap decision.

It is now being suggested to emergency room doctors by some baby battering experts that every suspected case of battering should immediately be hospitalized for further investigation, though whether or not the parents should be informed of the reason is under some dispute. Even in *Helping the Battered Child and his Family*, a symposium of chapters by various experts edited by Kempe and Helfer (1972), there is disagreement on this point. The editors suggest that the reason for this disagreement among their contributors is that they are writing about hospitals with differing capabilities. On the one hand there is the view that most doctors in emergency rooms are young and therefore inexperienced, both medically and in coping with emotionally charged situations. They will not be able, it is felt, to deal properly with such parents, so that this aspect of the problem ought to be left to those doctors experienced in such matters, the emergency doctors meanwhile concentrating on seeing that the children are instantly put in a safe ward where the cause of their injuries can be confirmed.

On the other hand there are those doctors who feel that if a child is clearly not suffering from an injury which needs in-patient treatment the parents will know this and it will not be possible to gull them into accepting the admission of their child into hospital without an adequate explanation. A young inexperienced doctor trying to fob the parents off with some lie or other is likely to cause even more mistrust and future prob-lems than if he had told the truth in the first place.

The answer here seems to be that everything depends on the hospital set-up. Where a consultant is always available, he will be able to discuss the matter properly with the parents, but in some hospitals there may be no one suitably qualified in the building. And even in the best-run hospitals consultants are not usually available during the night hours unless specially called out, so that in many cases everything must inevitably be left to the emergency doctor. It is a very difficult decision for him to make, whether or not to keep a child in, and whether or not to tell the parents the truth. His path must be eased as much as possible, and this can only be done by a very clear policy being laid down by his seniors.

After years of their experience in Colorado Helfer and Kempe now state categorically, 'All emergency room physicians must recognize that the suspected diagnosis of non-accidental injury to children mandates admission to the hospital, which will greatly facilitate the necessary diagnostic evaluation.' We have looked at some of the problems in which such admission would involve a young emergency doctor, but with the rate of rebat-tering as high as it is, it obviously makes sense that all sus-pected cases should immediately be admitted. It may prove highly embarrassing to insist on hospitalizing a child whose injuies would not seem to justify in-patient treatment, but better embarrassment than a child's death. At the moment it is not even mandatory in this country to report cases of suspected battering, so that it is perfectly possible for an emergency doctor to suspect battering, to patch up the injury, perhaps to write on a filing card the words 'suspected battering', and for that piece of information then to be filed away never to be seen again.

The problem arises as to how the emergency doctor can make sure he is not making a fool of himself and, worse, causing distress to innocent parents. Some ways of diagnosing a suspected case of battering will be explored later in this chapter, but I would like to reiterate that it has been estimated that 10 per cent of the children appearing in emergency rooms with traumatic injuries have been physically abused. With such a high number of likely cases, it becomes obvious that the ability to diagnose cases of child abuse is an immensely important part of a doctor's armoury, and one which every emergency doctor must be carefully taught. Medical readers of this book will find far more detail than I can quote here in *Helping the Battered Child and his Family*, and I would strongly recommend that they study the experience gained by their American counterparts.

Assuming we now have the child safely tucked up in his hospital bed, what is likely to happen to him then? Where there is a scheme such as that operating in Northampton the child will be examined by the consultant paediatrician and the police surgeon, complete skeletal X-rays will be made and the battering confirmed or otherwise. Since at the moment few children who are not severely battered are admitted to hospital the question is generally one of confirming how much damage has been done rather than if it has been done at all.

Many feel that it is more satisfactory for the child to be placed in a general ward if his injuries will permit this rather than for him to be isolated. A sensible hospital will keep the facts behind the injuries as secret as possible. Nurses untrained in this problem should not be informed, as it may be impossible for them to treat the parents as easily and sympathetically as they treat other parents. As one sister said to me, 'You mustn't let these parents think you are keeping an eye on them all the time – they have to be as free to come and go as other parents. It's not my place to accuse or inflict guilt on them, and it wouldn't help if I did. But you can't expect some of these young nurses to feel like that about it, so we tell them as little as possible.' If the nurses do find out, a sympathetic sister can help them to understand and accept the situation, but one can easily imagine how in some hospitals where such an attitude is not taken it would be virtually impossible for battering parents to continue visiting their children.

Equally, word must not be allowed to reach other visiting parents: if their own child is suffering a genuine accident or some severe illness they are likely to be very bitter indeed about parents who have 'deliberately' injured their own children. A psychiatrist working in a hospital which deals entirely with children says, however, that in the therapy sessions which his battering parents attend along with other parents who are suffering various emotional problems (often arising from at- tempting to cope unaided with chronically sick children), he finds no difficulties regarding sympathy. The general attitude in the therapy group is one of understanding, the typical com- ment being that they don't know how they don't do it them- selves. He finds that 'It's the so-called normal person who's forgotten his own wishes to bash who condemns these parents, people such as nurses, some doctors, police, those whose institu- tional roles have got something to do with welfare, these are the ones who are shocked.' This psychiatrist felt is might be wiser not to place such children in ordinary wards because of this attitude, which might cause damage to parents who are very easily upset by feelings of rejection. 'If we're going to get anywhere with helping them we have to protect these parents from *our* feelings, and you can't expect ordinary ward staff to disguise their own reactions very efficiently. In an ordinary paediatric ward I think it might be better to separate them, but not in a psychiatric ward – people there would understand and be willing to help.'

In severe cases even experienced doctors and nurses will occasionally find themselves reacting so strongly they may have difficulty in controlling themselves. Battering parents are fre- quently suspicious, cantakerous people, easily upset, varying between obsequiousness and a stubborn refusal to cooperate.

Those whose job it is to tend the body of a bruised and scarred baby may find it is almost beyond them at times to speak patiently and kindly with a parent who seems set on being as dislikeable as possible. Case conferences, where such bitterness can be aired and true feelings admitted to understanding colleagues, are a source of help in these circumstances.

In a hospital setting the people most likely to attend these case conferences are the paediatricians looking after the baby, the sister in charge of the children's ward, the hospital social worker and sometimes the social worker from the parent's area, the NSPCC if they have been involved, the parent's GP if he wishes to come, and a psychiatrist if one is attached to the hospital or if either of the parents is already under the care of one. In the few areas where the police are actively involved they will also be represented.

These conferences are meant to review the past and future treatment of the parent and the child and to decide whether or not action ought to be taken against the parents, though at the first conference the primary interest will be in treating the child. In hospitals aware of the problems involved, care will be taken to keep these discussions informal and private, the resultant notes being kept locked up apart from ordinary medical files so that they cannot be read by some unauthorized person merely out of curiosity.

In some hospitals the system works well; the parents are kept in the picture, they are helped at home by social workers who also attend the hospital case conference, and eventually the child is able to be returned to them. But in others there seems to be a serious lack of coordination. The cured child is returned home without anyone having ensured its future safety, or perhaps the parents insist on removing the child and no one in the hospital takes the necessary steps to prevent this happening. Some hospitals have arranged with their local social services or police that a care order restricting the parents' rights may be placed on a child within a matter of hours if it is felt necessary to do so. Other hospitals say they are unable to keep a child in hospital if the parents wish otherwise, and appear to make no effort to thwart the parents. Arrangements to obtain care orders easily must be made in advance at every hospital against the eventuality that a parent will want to remove a child before the family is considered ready to receive the child back. Even if the child has fully recovered from his injuries he must not be returned too early, or he will probably be back in hospital within a few weeks, suffering from a worse injury than the first time. No effort ought to be spared to ensure that a child is not allowed home until everyone concerned feels the right moment has arrived.

Deciding when that time has come is one of the most important decisions any doctor has to make. Some hospitals take the advice of psychiatrists, others do not. How helpful the opinions of psychiatrists are in this situation is something that has not yet been proved, but the general feeling seems to be that most psychiatrists at present still favour a more rapid return to the parents than do some of the other workers involved, although this Bowlby-inspired reaction does seem to be weakening. The Maria Colwell case will probably quicken the decline of the popular notion that almost any parent is better than any substitute, a mistaken idea which has been responsible for much tragedy in the past.

Psychiatrists working in the field of child care who are up to date in their reading have probably mostly moved on from the position Bowlby did so much to popularize in the 1950s, and even during the two years I have spent working on this book I have noticed a definite swing away from the idea that nearly all children should be returned, even among those workers who had seemed to me committed to this view to the point of naïvety. Kempe's recent comments have no doubt helped here : 'If the home cannot be made safe (i.e., to maintain the child free from repeated physical injury) . . . a therapeutic failure must be admitted and, in all fairness to the child and his parents, parental rights may have to be severed.' He estimates this failure rate to be about 25 per cent, a higher figure than was previously supposed.

Slightly fewer than 10 per cent of the parents are seriously mentally ill, psychotics or aggressive psychopaths who will not respond to the kind of treatment usually effective with other battering parents. But beyond this 10 per cent Kempe now accepts that there are another 15 per cent who in spite of treatment still cannot be considered as safe parents. Pollock and Steele write (in *Helping the Battered Child and his Family*): 'Under the best of conditions we would estimate that at least 80 per cent of cases can be treated with reasonably satisfactory results', but the words 'under the best of conditions' probably account for the difference in numbers here. If 90 per cent of the parents may be taken to be comparatively normal (i.e., not psychopathic or psychotic), then perhaps in the future the 75 to 80 per cent success rate may be improved, but for the moment it must be borne in mind that in about a quarter of all cases coming to light the child will eventually have to be removed from its home.

Sentimental assumptions about parents' rights and natural ties must not be allowed to interfere with a decision which should be made by a committee sufficiently expert to be able to ensure as near as humanly possible that a mistake is not made. Such a decision should never be left in the hands of one or two people, whose prejudices or lack of experience may well result in the death of a child whose life ought to have been saved. Helfer has estimated that a child who is returned home after injury without further action being taken to aid the parents, stands a 25 to 50 per cent chance of being either killed or permanently injured. Since much of the aid given at present is woefully inadequate, one wonders what the figures might be even amongst those who are supposed to be receiving care. If the committee were automatically to follow up at regular intervals all cases which had passed through their hands, even in areas where the social services labour under almost intolerable strains, such extra attention might make all the difference between life and death for many children.

Anyone can recognize a battered child bearing the typical stigmata – fractured skull, bruised and cut face, X-rays revealing previous lesions – but such injuries as these are the result of an advanced stage of battering which, if the diagnosis of early or even pre-battering stages could be improved, in many cases never need be reached at all. The last decade of research has resulted in considerable progress in the prognosis of battering, and already the number of serious cases in relation to mild cases appears to be dropping, although there is an overall increase in both owing to the increased rate of reporting.

As we have seen, failure to diagnose or to report suspected battering will almost inevitably result in further attacks. We know the rebattering rate is very high – at least 60 per cent – and the actual rate, including comparatively minor attacks which are either not severe enough to need treatment or which are treated but their cause not realized, is probably even higher. Of course, some cases of battering simply cannot be proved, and a family may remain under suspicion while 'accident' follows 'accident' without any action being taken. I was told by several policemen and women of various cases which they felt certain were instances of deliberate child abuse but which they had never been able to prove; children would mysteriously fall through narrow gaps in windows which they could only have reached by clever gymnastics, probably – but not provably – beyond their ability; successive children in a family would swallow aspirin or medicine in lethal and sub-lethal doses; small infants would tumble into nearly boiling baths, for which 'accident' an older sibling might be blamed. Genuine accidents of this kind do undoubtedly happen, and a policeman's hunch that any particular incident is no accident is not enough grounds for action. Proof of guilt in such cases is very hard to come by. Sometimes three or four children in a family will receive such injuries, some of them to the point of death, before action is finally taken. An accusation of neglect is all that may be fastened on the parents even then, but in such circumstances this will be enough to separate any remaining children from their parents. Even then no one can be a hundred per cent certain that all such accidents in the family were not genuinely accidental, the result of criminal carelessness but not of criminal assault.

Even in more obvious cases of battering the correct diagnosis is not always made or it may be found more convenient to hope the parent has learned his or her lesson and will not attack again. Let us look at two brief cases from the NSPCC's *Retrospective Study* (1969): 'In a social record relating to the third child in a family, there are notes about two older siblings. The first child died from head injuries. The second child was injured in unknown circumstances which cast considerable suspicion on the mother. The third child, when nine weeks old, was treated for a fractured femur. This fracture was noted when the child, who had been born with talipes, was taken to hospital to have a plaster changed on his leg. He was discharged home. A week following his discharge he was admitted with a fractured skull.'

In the second case a baby was repeatedly taken to the same hospital for treatment. At two months old it was treated for a fracture of the right femur (thigh-bone), and was then discharged home. Five weeks later he was returned with a new fracture in the same place, but no adequate explanation was given. In spite of the improbability of such a small baby breaking its own leg, he was once more discharged home. Six months later he was brought in critically ill with a fractured skull, his right femur fractured for the third time.

Bruising in older children who can run and climb may be a less obvious symptom than fractured limbs, but how many tiny babies suffer genuine accidental bruising? Again the *Retrospective Study* quotes various cases: 'Age 3 weeks: child treated for bruises to the face. 5 weeks later – fractured skull.' 'Age 2 months: rib fractures treated in hospital. 5 months later – bruises treated in hospital. 2 months later – further bruising treated at clinic and further bruising treated at hospital . . .' The list of bruising continues, the report concluding laconically that 'the record is still active'.

Lastly, a third case: 'Age 7 months: child taken to doctor with bruises. Mother reports that she was told they were not serious. 2 weeks later – fatal head injury.'

These are all typical and many similar cases could be quoted, some ending in brutal attacks resulting in death. Clearly, not only is better diagnosis needed, but also an efficient system whereby hospitals can check with general practitioners and other hospitals if a child has suffered a previous injury. If such a check were automatic for every injury regardless of explanation then many lives would be saved. In America reporting of all suspected baby battering cases is mandatory, though there seems to be some confusion at present as to who should receive the report. Such a law ought to be passed here without delay. The NSPCC has repeatedly stressed the importance of a national register, and in the light of publicity surrounding the Maria Colwell case it seems likely that the NSPCC's advice will at last be taken.

Attempts at keeping local registers have been made in some counties, but without legal enforcement most have turned out to be very patchy affairs indeed. Sometimes it is the social services who have tried to organize a register, on which they have entered the name of any child suspected of being in possible danger through poverty, severe marital discord or other causes of stress which might disrupt a home. Elsewhere it has been the Medical Officer of Health or one of his assistants who has begun the register.

One such doctor talked to me about her register which was restricted to children up to three years of age who had suffered any injury, accidental or otherwise. When the register was first begun she found general enthusiasm, with information coming from many quarters. Soon, however, the supply tailed off and now is mostly restricted to information from local hospitals about babies who have been actually battered. But the main object of such a register is not to record such details but to list the names of every injured child no matter how the injury occurred, so that those whose names have appeared previously may have their background checked by visiting social workers. This doctor found that information comes in spurts: when a new casualty doctor starts at a hospital he is told of the system and at first he willingly sends along the required details. But after the first three or four notices his enthusiasm vanishes and nothing more is heard from the emergency department until a new replacement takes over, when the same process is repeated. A few cases are reported to her by general practitioners, and occasionally a health visitor tells her of a possible case, but the list is so far from complete as to be virtually useless. She agrees that at present it is unlikely that she will receive the kind of complete cooperation which she would like, but she sees no reason why everyone concerned could not take the trouble at least to report every case of any severity – bad burns, fractures, cases of failure to thrive, or severe bruising.

Such a list would be a powerful aid for social workers: at present they may visit a family regularly, and yet have no idea that one or even all of its children have been taken, possibly on several occasions, to various hospitals for out-patient treatment. Case after case is reported of social workers, on being asked how it was they had repeatedly visited a family without noticing signs of battering, replying that the child concerned had not been seen by them for several months because they were told it had been asleep when they called, or that it was at a neighbour's, or out somewhere playing. They have accepted these excuses as genuine, not wishing to upset the mother by letting her suppose she was distrusted, or even simply because they did not want to inconvenience her. A register would at least let these social workers know which children are in possible danger, and might help to stiffen the more gentle or timid of them to the point where they will refuse to accept any excuse and insist on seeing the child for themselves.

Such a register would also be of inestimable value to doctors, and ought to be easily available to general practitioners. However, serious injuries to tiny babies may occur before their name has been entered on any list: perhaps each doctor ought to keep his own private file in which he enters the name of every mother who brings in her baby for any reason whatsoever, except in cases of clearly defined diseases like chicken pox or streaming colds. The more trivial the reason for the visit, the more important it is that the child's name should be entered. He could then check very quickly each time a baby is brought in and determine for himself if the reasons for bringing the child are of the type a parent might use when making a 'cry for help'. If so, he ought to take particular pains with the mother, and immediately on her departure contact a health visitor. If she feels his suspicions might be justified the child's name ought then to be circulated to local hospitals so that in the event of an attack, however minor, preventive action can immediately be taken. Obviously, absolute confidentiality is of extreme importance here : great damage would be done if such a list could be seen by any casual hospital worker living locally who happened to feel curious.

The general practitioner and the child welfare clinics need to look out not only for such cries for help and the more obvious cases of bruising, etc., but also for the symptoms of what is known as 'a failure to thrive'. The growth of most babies falls within a recognizable pattern, and where a baby is gaining insufficient weight and height he is diagnosed as a case of failure to thrive. There can be many reasons for this, but it is being recognized more and more as a possible symptom of pre-battering or as allied to actual physical battering.

It was explained earlier that most battering parents do in fact look after their babies from a general point of view very well; but there are some who through incompetence or other reasons do not feed their babies sufficiently or properly. In other cases it may be that emotional deprivation is behind the failure to thrive, although there is doubt about this in some quarters. Certainly many under-developed babies taken into hospital do thrive very well under proper care, rapidly putting on weight in spite of being deprived of the love and personal attention one might expect them to receive at home. Of course this success can have very dangerous results : if the nurses looking after the child succeed in making the mother feel incompetent, briskly proving to her that the child's poor growth was *her* fault and not the child's, then once she has it home again she is likely out of shame and frustration to bash up the child as soon as she runs into the first feeding problem.

In cases such as this, extreme tact is needed on the part of the nurses and the doctors dealing with the child. Kempe has said,

'You must supplement loving in a case like this. You must give the mother additional loving, as well as the baby. You can do this by home help, part-time nurseries, or by mothers' groups. Some women are adequate as half-time mothers, but they can't make it for the other half so we must supplement it. It's much cheaper all round than having the child in care.'

The truth is that the phrase 'baby battering' covers a confusingly wide spectrum of problems, from simple 'failure to thrive', through 'accidental' poisoning, to fractures of limbs and skull, and fatal damage to the brain. What help does a doctor have in trying to decide what diagnosis to make? There have been various technical papers published by doctors experienced in the syndrome, listing in detail typical injuries, and no doubt in the next few years there will be many more. The bibliography lists some of the papers published so far, but for the benefit of non-medical readers I will outline some of the symptoms, although a book of this nature is not the place for lengthy medical detail.

First of all it must be made clear that many of the injuries are indistinguishable from those caused by genuine accidents, and therefore it is often difficult to be certain of their origin. In a study by Gregg and Elmer, out of 146 children who were X-rayed after injury, 30 were from families which were judged to be abusive. Yet eleven of these children had had accidents which were perfectly credible. As Carolyn Okell writes: 'In some instances unconscious motives in the parent . . . seem to be linked with accidental injuries sustained by their young children. For example . . . mothers have continually exposed their young children to danger by leaving them unsupervised at the top of a flight of stairs or with the side of the cot down, and the children have received a series of injuries. This could well be interpreted as an expression of unconscious hostility.'

Poisoning is another instance: how do you tell when a bottle of aspirin or medicine has been deliberately or half-deliberately left in an available place? At what point does carelessness become 'unconscious hostility'? Some people are naturally incautious, and a bottle left on a table may be nothing more than sheer forgetfulness. However, writing as a naturally untidy person myself, I know from my own experience that having a baby forces one to change many of one's ways; certainly I found myself becoming almost over-cautious about things like hygiene and bottles of medicine, electric points and sharp knives, to compensate for my own natural habits. Nevertheless large numbers of small children are poisoned every year; where it is not genuinely accidental some doctors will not label such deaths 'baby battering', but prefer to use the word 'murder'. Others disagree and say it is all part of the same syndrome, merely a different method of attack. Personally I feel that if the phrase 'baby battering' is going to be extended to children suffering from burns and failure-to-thrive babies, then it should also be extended to cases of poisoning through 'carelessness'.

One of the first positive signs which a doctor may pick up is that the parents' timing is peculiar. He may know from examining the child that the parents have lied about the time of the accident, or they may quite openly admit the delay, but nearly always there *is* some delay, sometimes only a matter of hours, sometimes as much as two or three days, before the child is presented for treatment. Another sign which may be helpful is the child's general attitude. Sometimes the baby will appear very frightened, cowering away from anyone trying to touch it. But this is not always the case, some children behaving in a pattern perfectly normal for their age group.

Earlier in this chapter, on page 155, we noted that one study has suggested that bruising and fractures are far more common than lacerations, which makes a useful pointer for diagnosis. The NSPCC figures show that injuries to the face and head are much more likely than injuries to other parts of the body (73 per cent against 27 per cent), which seems to imply that these parents wanted to be stopped and therefore chose to attack areas of the body which could be seen. Who can fail to notice a child with a black eye?

Injuries to the mouth are highly typical. Cameron writes: 'The presence, in almost 50 per cent of cases, of laceration of the mucosa of the inner aspect of the upper lip, near the frenulum, sometimes with tearing of the lip from the alveolar margin of the gum, is now considered almost pathognomonic. This injury is thought to be the result of a blow on the mouth or of other efforts to silence a screaming or crying child.'

Two forensic doctors told me they had noticed an increase lately in bite marks. One remarked that fashions seem to change: a few years back there was a rash of babies with identical injuries which he soon learned to recognize as the mark of a stiletto heel ground into the stomach. With the demise of the stiletto heel, bite marks, previously rare, have become more common. Biting has strong love-hate overtones, and it may possibly be that the opening up of sexual frankness in public debate has allowed a more open physical expression of the frustrated love such parents often seem to feel. Such bites have sometimes led to easy proof as to who the attacker was: a missing tooth or a ragged set of lower teeth can occasionally be identified in the injury and the culprit recognized beyond doubt.

Eye damage has been found to be very often associated with battering, owing to the frequency of attacks to the head. In small children such damage may not be noted at first, so a careful examination of all battered babies ought to take into account the possibility of retinal haemorrhage. Equally, where a child is known to be suffering from such damage, the possibility of battering ought to be considered.

Burns mostly occur where they can be seen, though not all are. A sudden stab with a cigarette end, dropping the baby into an over-hot bath, pushing it against an electric fire or paraffin heater, sitting the child on a hot oven: the causes of many burns are difficult to identify but they rarely match the inadequate reasons given. Such details as these shock, and tend to negate any sympathy one might otherwise feel for the parent. But against this must be set the extraordinary fact that the child will then be brought to a doctor for attention: Mrs Jones burned Paul quite deliberately on the hand but nevertheless took him to her health visitor the same day for the blister to be dressed. This was quite unnecessary: it was a small blister and Mrs Jones was more than capable of looking after it herself.

Her motivations must have been very mixed: guilt, desire to ease her conscience, a need for sympathy from the nurse, all of these certainly but also an undoubted love for Paul, a desire to make him well again and, above all, a desperate need to make someone recognize what was happening and stop her from doing such a thing again.

The most severe injuries are likely to be damage to the brain or abdomen, such as bruising of the intestines or a rupture of the liver resulting from a kick or a punch, or even jumping up and down on the prostrate child. Sometimes minor bruises on a child's body may reveal, for example, just how he was held while being hit against a table. Dr Hall in an address to the Royal Society of Health in April 1972 elaborated at length how to recognize these and other bruises, explaining how thumb and finger marks are typically displayed, and also stressing that bruises which may appear unidentifiable frequently form a recognizable pattern if a child is placed in the position in which he happened to be when attacked. A child lying stretched out on its side may show what appears to be a random collection of bruises, but if the legs are drawn up in a foetal position it may clearly be seen that the bruises form a straight line where a child was beaten with a stick.

Grip marks are particularly revealing: 'On the forehead the basic pattern is a larger bruise over the right eye and a crop of several smaller bruises on the left side of the forehead. . . . When a hand is used to span the marks they conform, with ease, to the thumb and fingers of the examiner.' Bruises on the legs are more difficult to be certain about as most normal children's legs bear some, but groups of fingertip marks are often found by the knees or the elbows where a child has been gripped prior to hurling it across a room or while shaking it violently. Since new injuries to the bones do not always immediately show up on X-rays, recognition of suspicious bruising is a very important aid to diagnosis. Fresh X-rays should be taken two or three weeks later, after which interval new bone formation may now be visible.

The pulling and heavy handling that such children sometimes

receive often causes fractures of long bones and internal hae-morrhages, which go unremarked and untreated. However, these old injuries in various stages of repair will show up in X-rays, confirming suspicions already aroused by the combination of heavy bruising, the parent's delay in reporting the new injury, and the inadequate excuses given, such as 'she fell down-stairs', 'he fell out of his cot', 'a swing hit him in the tummy', 'her brother dropped his toy truck onto her stomach', 'it just come up all on its own in the night'.

This brief list of injuries can only give some idea of what should be looked out for, and it would repay interested doctors to study the detailed diagnostic findings in the various papers available. Recognition of bruising patterns is of immense impor-tance in the early stages of battering if this kind of injuring is to be avoided : 'approximately 40 per cent of fatal cases will be found to have a subdural haemorrhage with or without a frac-tured skull, and at the same time, in many cases, there will be compression of the chest with fractured ribs and ruptured vis-cera (internal organs). Rupture of the liver and abdominal vis-cera . . . is seen but external bruising of the abdominal wall is not necessarily present : a reminder that a diffuse blow to the relaxed abdomen may cause severe internal injury and yet leave no external mark' (Cameron, 1972).

It will never be possible to save every child from death : there will always be the occasional case where unexpected stress has a sudden and violent effect on the parent of a very small baby with immediate disastrous results. But in the majority of cases there is some warning, time for action to be taken. Where every doctor, every nurse, every health visitor is familiar with every symptom of battering, the majority of cases, which at present progress through various stages of battering, may be caught in time before serious damage is done. Is that not a worthwhile goal to aim for?

A valuable weapon in the doctor's armoury would be an ability to detect the possibility that an as-yet innocent patient might batter at some time in the future. Such techniques are at present being explored in America, and in the next chapter some of the results obtained from these studies will be discussed. They are still in an experimental stage, but they have already thrown up many interesting ideas which should be of use to everyone whose primary aim is to stop battering even before it begins.

Chapter 8
The parents

Until a scientific experiment has been successfully repeated several times by different researchers, its results are not taken to be finally established. Few investigations into the pattern of baby battering have been submitted to such rigorous retesting. Nevertheless one grasps eagerly at the results of any properly-based research, particularly those stemming from the work carried out over the last ten years at the University of Colorado. Of especial interest were the results obtained when Kempe and his fellow-workers made a predictive study of a thousand normal mothers who came to their Obstretrics Clinic as part of a perfectly ordinary post-natal routine. If battering parents can be identified at an early stage much suffering can be avoided.

Working on their belief that 20 per cent of women experience some difficulty in mastering the art of mothering, their investigation took note of the 200 or so mothers who seemed to them to fall in this category. They narrowed this group of 20 per cent down to a hundred mothers, about whom they felt fairly serious concern. They then split this further sample into two, using one group of fifty as a control group. To the remaining fifty they gave consistent help, arranging for weekly visits in their homes by mothering aids and so on. Their findings were that none of the mothers who were being helped assaulted their children, whereas of the control group, three children were battered and one was killed.

What questions did they ask to identify the potential batterers? The questions were fairly simple, obvious enough when you consider their implications; nevertheless few people would think of asking them of a young mother. They asked things like: 'Do you get angry at the new baby? Do you feel people are critical of the way you take care of the baby? Are you frightened to be alone with a baby?' Many ordinary young mothers are going to answer yes to at least one or two of these questions, and it takes the right answers to several different groups of questions before one can feel fairly certain that one is dealing with a mother who is going to have more than the normal difficulty in adjusting to new motherhood. Other revealing questions might be: 'Do your older children understand your problems? Do they take care of you?' Or, 'How does your mother feel about her new grandchild? Does she think you are handling motherhood well?'

When questions such as these are followed by ones about discipline, attitudes become clearer. If a mother feels that it is possible to spank a three- or four-week-old baby in order to make it behave properly then you are dealing with an abnormal situation. Parents who believe discipline at such an early age is not only needful but possible, and who consider an eight-week-old baby is capable of being deliberately naughty, are in danger of battering their child and they need supportive care. Not all doctors or social workers, however, are capable of asking the right questions in the right way and of arriving at the right answers.

In order to overcome these difficulties three American doctors (Schneider, Helfer and Pollock) have been trying to develop a foolproof questionnaire which will predict parents with a battering potential, but it is not an easy project. Parents tend to give the answers they believe are wanted, or they may reply with what they genuinely imagine to be the truth. How to get them to delve into their deeply-buried feelings is the real problem. The answer seems to lie in a highly sophisticated questionnaire with various clusters of statements which the parent marks on a 7 point scale, ranging from 'strongly agree' to 'strongly disagree', so that although a normal parent might respond to some of the questions as would a potential batterer, he would not complete the full combination of answers which would reveal his child to be in danger. The work done so far on the formation of such a questionnaire is highly promising, and it is hoped that soon it will have passed the developmental stage. For those interested in further details the study is fully described in an Appendix in *Helping the Battered Child and his Family*.

One of the difficulties experienced in attempting to arrive at a useful state of communication with these parents is that in the past words have not been very helpful to them, and consequently they continue to mistrust them in their adulthood. It has been suggested that their personalities have been fixated at a very early stage of their development when behaviour patterns were more important than verbal communication. Proof that someone really does care what happens to them needs to be shown physically by workers visiting them in their own houses, by aiding them with their own hands, showing by touch and look that they actually mean the words their mouths utter. No matter how often the worker is rebuffed she must persevere until the client begins to have trust in her.

A person who has no consistent sense of his own identity needs to gain an image of himself from the way other people see him. Having been faced all his life by his parent's poor concept of him, he may be thoroughly confused by the good picture a social worker will be trying to present, and may repeatedly try to destroy this new image of himself by breaking appointments, rudeness or some childish form of petulance. He wants to be socially successful, particularly as a parent, and will sometimes be able to function as a loving, wise father. But this concept of himself is very shaky, and he can change only too swiftly to the role of punitive parent (learnt from his own father). He has a collection of disparate ideas about who he is, and who he wants to be, but no one clear image of himself as a mature man, so that he is very easily thrown by some mildly stressful event that would not cause a more stable personality the slightest disturbance.

That these parents have no confidence in their own ability to do anything successfully is hardly remarkable when you consider that their own parents continuously scolded them for their inadequacy as children, never giving them a feeling of pleasure or pride in themselves. Frequently they were not even allowed friends of their own choosing since their parents were jealous and wanted to keep them close. New friends would be denigrated or prohibited outright, so how could they develop any form of social ease or trust in others?

It may seem over-simple to keep harking back to their childhood, but it must be remembered that many of these battering parents have only recently left it behind. The NSPCC found that 73 out of 286 battering mothers were aged between sixteen and twenty, while a further 140 were aged between twenty-one and twenty-five, making a total of 74 per cent under twenty-five years of age. Fathers were almost as young: out of 243, 34 were aged between sixteen and twenty, and 97 were aged between twenty-one and twenty-five. The average ages of the total sample was 23.59 years for the mothers, and 26.7 for the fathers (a smaller sample described in the 1969 report showed each group to be even younger, by an average of eighteen months each). Interestingly, Selwyn Smith and his colleagues, researching on battering parents at the Queen Elizabeth Hospital in Birmingham, found an identical figure for their mothers, who averaged 23.5 years also. Additionally, they point out that these mothers on average had given birth to their first child at 19½, whereas the national average age is just over 23 for a first birth.

For the younger mothers at least, many of their old school mates will still be buying unlimited clothes, make-up, pop magazines and the latest top-of-the-pops disc, and perhaps more important will be going out dancing and to the cinema with a variety of boy-friends who have plenty of money in their pockets. The young mother instead is trapped in some small flat or in the in-laws' house with a squalling baby and a young husband who is every bit as discontented as she is. Is it any wonder some of the more immature snap under the strain?

One might expect such mothers to go out to work as soon as possible, not only to earn extra money but also to get out of the house, but in fact it seems few battering mothers do so. The NSPCC found that only three out of seventy-seven mothers in their 1969 sample went out to work, and these findings agree with those of other researchers, both in England and in America. It seems that these mothers have such an emotional dependency on their children they will not entrust them to another's care so that they may go out working; indeed, this refusal to be parted from their babies is one of the problems doctors have to face if they attempt to keep a child in hospital.

What sort of personalities do these parents have? Are they usually intelligent or stupid? Questions such as these are being researched and the general picture is becoming clearer, although there is still much to learn. Sometimes they are depressed passive people, overtly seeking the support and affection of their children, perhaps competing with their spouses for their children's love, or vice versa. Others are cold to their families and make extreme demands which are impossible to fulfil; often they show compulsive traits such as fanatical tidiness or cleanliness. Both these types show many similarities : they are incomplete personalities who have been deprived of mothering and wish to make up this deficiency in their own families but are incapable of doing so. The resulting behaviour pattern was discussed at some length in chapter 2, and will not be gone into again here.

The second basic type consists of those whose aggressiveness is the dominant thing about them. Skinner and Castle write in their *Retrospective Study* (1969) : 'Forty-seven per cent of the sample comprising twenty-five men and ten women were characterized by essentially anti-social behaviour of the predominantly aggressive type. There were indications that these adults were habitually aggressive and that their behaviour tended to be released against any source of irritation. Many of them had criminal records and were prone to violent outbursts of temper in the home. They displayed a readiness to enter into conflict with authority and all their personal relationships were stormy.'

Nevertheless, it has been found that many of these people can be helped successfully, although it is not possible to eradicate entirely their ingrained aggressiveness. Selwyn Smith and his fellow researchers have been exploring the organic condition of parents, as they considered that insufficient attention had been paid to this side of the problem. On examining the electro-encephalograms of thirty self-admitted baby batterers they found that eight had abnormal EEG patterns, and all these eight admitted they persistently hit one or more of their children. They therefore conclude that some parents batter because they are organically disposed to violence regardless of whether or not stress exists. Of their sample as a whole (214 parents of battered children) they found that one-third of the fathers had a gross personality defect and that nearly half of the mothers were neurotic. However they classified only a minority as being obviously mentally ill and felt that since the injuries these particular parents inflicted were so clearly of a highly bizarre nature they ought to be considered quite separately from the rest.

Ray Castle, while accepting the results of the electroencephalogram tests, comments that although it may be true that in some cases the problem is an organic rather than a nurturing or an environmental one, nevertheless the parents they have been looking after at their Research Department, even when of an aggressive type, do respond to treatment, and their children have been able to remain at home. He feels that whatever the cause, early help, if effective and continuous, will save the situation (except in the case of psychopaths and psychotics).

Another interesting finding of the Birmingham researchers was that nearly one-third of the fathers in the sample had a criminal record, while Skinner and Castle found in their NSPCC sample that 45 per cent of the fathers and over 9 per cent of the mothers had known criminal records. They point out that in the country as a whole the expected rates of the incidence of indictable offences for the age group of twenty-one to thirty years during the same period was 1·9 per cent for males and 0·2 per cent for females. However, the NSPCC deals in the main with a socially restricted class of poorer people, and their figures would probably not hold true for a sample taken from the community as a whole. Nevertheless there seems no doubt that the criminal record of battering parents is higher than the national average.

The intelligence of these parents is the subject of much debate. Selwyn Smith found that the subjects with abnormal

EEGs had low intelligence; indeed he found that nearly half of the mothers in his sample were of subnormal intelligence. It is frequently suggested that it is the less bright who physically batter, while the more intelligent inflict mental battering, which may in the long run be more disastrous. At present there are simply not enough data to prove anything, but there is no question that plenty of very intelligent people do physically batter their children. It may be that they are caught less often, however, being capable of lying their way out of a situation more convincingly. This is yet another side of battering which needs more research, for the American findings show very different results from the English ones, probably owing to the wider class coverage of parents seen by the researchers. Steele and Pollock write in *The Battered Child* (1968), 'There is no evidence of a significant relationship between intelligence as measured by intelligence tests and abuse. The IQs obtained by the patients seen for testing range between 73 and 130, with most of the patients faling into the average range (90–110).'

The question of class and intelligence has been hotly debated, and any new books by Eysenck or Herrnstein, for example, are certain to spark off fresh controversy. Whatever stance one takes on this subject, however, no one is going to deny that there are plenty of bright people in the lower social classes and plenty of stupid ones in the upper classes. The intelligent, regardless of their class, will probably be better at hiding the situation if they are battering their children. Not only will they be abe to offer more convincing excuses, but in many more cases they may see their needs more clearly and be able to obtain outside aid more easily. If they are rich enough they may send their children to boarding school or hire nannies if they do not have them already, they can go to restful health farms or manage an extra holiday abroad, they will take frequent weekends off with their spouses and will generally be able to opt out of the situation. The stupid rich have the same advantages, and can pay for advisers to arrange for them what they are unable to do for themselves. The NSPCC will not be called in, the health visitor will not come knocking at their door, and not a soul except their doctor, their psychiatrist and perhaps an intimate friend or two will ever know anything has happened. The stupid poor will enter the statistics, however, and it is mostly this group about whom we all read in reports. But let us not be misled into thinking that this is purely a lower-class problem arising among the mentally subnormal, whatever the statistics seem to prove.

Admittedly, it is possible that if every single case of mild battering were to be followed up throughout the entire country (though this could never happen as much of it would never be suspected by anyone) it might be found that a higher percentage of poor people eventually progress to severe battering than do rich people. There are still many who live in appalling conditions, deprived of physical comforts taken for granted by most of us; for thousands more, a minor crisis such as a lost overcoat, which would mean little to a well-off family, can assume disastrous proportions when money is really short. The rich cannot only afford to buy their way out of a dangerous situation, they never even begin to experience the strain under which some people pass their entire lives.

Nevertheless, mental anguish is not the prerogative of the poor, and well-off children can still be maimed emotionally even if they escape severe battering more frequently than poorer children. Several people suggested to me that these are the children who when they are a little older come up before the Juvenile Court for stealing, for example, and everybody asks, how can this nice middle-class boy have done such a thing – he must have got in with a bad set. Again, the upper-class boy will most likely avoid even this disgrace : I am not for a moment suggesting corruption, but a boy at a famous public school who is caught filching from a local shop will probably end up in front of his headmaster rather than a magistrate. He will be punished, but it is likely to be a less public punishment than a less well-off lad might expect.

My point, however, is that although money, together with the know-how that membership of the middle and upper classes brings, may help an actual or potential battering parent to avoid serious assaults, nevertheless the preliminary stages of battering are thought to be as endemic in these classes as in the poorer classes. There are many known cases of actual severe assault among the wealthy, although I have never seen such a case publicly discussed. I have been told of several myself by those personally involved, and know them to be true. Aristocratic families of famous title, highly respectable families living at 'excellent' addresses, good bourgeois parents whose lives seem admirable on the surface, behind all these façades there occasionally occur scenes as brutal and horrific as in any slum.

Sometimes a nanny will know her charge is being 'punished' to the point of severe injury, but will go along with the parent's explanation to the doctor in order to keep her job; at other times it is the nanny herself who does the battering. I was told of one case where such a nanny was found to have caused the child severe injuries. Because of the family's connections no one wanted publicity, so she was quietly dismissed. It is now known that she is working again as nanny to another family, but no one has taken any action against her. She appears to be a first-rate nurse, trustworthy and good with children : since she always denied that it was she who was the culprit, to accuse her again to her new employers might raise fresh unwanted publicity. Perhaps she will never batter again; who knows?

Battering parents long to have a child who will bring them credit and who will shine above all others : in the upper classes where most children anyway are submitted to the polishing process at an early age this demand can quickly amount to cruelty where a potential battering situation already exists. One such mother in her thirties told me how from four years onwards she was given French lessons, bridge lessons, dancing and etiquette lessons, her progress being checked each afternoon by her mother. If she was less than perfect she would be beaten. If she refused to apologize for not having learned her lessons properly she would continue to be beaten more and more severely all afternoon if necessary. A stubborn child, she took a certain perverse pleasure in defying her mother; the situation continued for years until her parents' marriage broke up and she was sent away to school. At the time several other people knew what was going on – her father, her nanny and other staff – but she was generally considered a difficult child and no one chose to interfere. She told me that when her own son was small she hated him when he cried, and sometimes she had an intense desire to kill him. Now that the child is older the family seems happy enough, but she willingly admits that if she had not been able to buy help and occasional freedom away from her baby when she needed it she almost certainly would have severely assaulted him when he was a baby.

There are undoubtedly many such cases, but mostly they remain unreported in the press. Their own doctors usually cannot bring themselves to suspect patients such as these, and I was told of many case histories by hospital doctors and others who found their work complicated by the refusal of some medical practitioners to believe in the guilt of such people. It *is* difficult to believe that battering is going on in a comfortably-off, educated household, when the parents, on the surface at least, are obviously self-controlled and self-aware people.

One man who had been frequently beaten by his father, a perfectionist with an unpredictable temper, said that once he and his brother screamed so loudly when they were being hit that their neighbours (who must already have guessed something of the situation) called in the NSPCC. However, 'By the time the NSPCC officer had been shown into our somewhat splendid hall by the maid and waited while my mother flowed very grandly down the stairs towards him, he must have lost some of his nerve. The maid said mother looked down her nose at him, told him she'd never heard such a lot of nonsense in her life and sent him packing. Certainly he never came back. My mother always backed up my father, you see.'

The NSPCC's figures for the social classes of the parents discussed in their two studies are as follows the first figure in the percentage recorded in their *Retrospective Study* (1969), the second in their 1972 study) : I Professional 0 per cent, 0 per cent; II Intermediate 0 per cent, 2·6 per cent; III Skilled manual 26 per cent, 18 per cent; IV Semi-skilled manual 9 per cent, 23·1 per cent; V Unskilled 54 per cent, 48·7 per cent; VI Unclassifiable 11 per cent, 7·6 per cent. However, they themselves comment that other studies show that battering occurs among classes I and II and that there is not thought to be any correlation between social class and child battering. Pollock and Steele (in *Helping the Battered Child and his Family*, 1972) specifically state that parents who physically attack their children come from all social levels. In considering the treatment and prevention of battering, therefore, it must not be forgotten that this problem is spread throughout all society, and that propaganda must reach every level. A child suffers no less because he happens to be comfortably-off as well as unhappy.

The problem of unemployment was discussed in Chapter 2. It is enough to add here that in the NSPCC's *Retrospective Study* of 1969 over 38 per cent of the fathers were unemployed, while the 1972 study showed that 22 per cent were. They add that both figures were far higher than the then current national unemployment figures. In various American studies a percentage above the national average of families were shown to be receiving financial help from public welfare departments. These facts imply that there is generally a high degree of unemployment among battering families. However, it must be remembered that these parents have a reputation for being nomadic, they have difficulty in relating to other people, they lack confidence in themselves and their ability to carry out a job properly, and if they are of the aggressive type they are liable to argue or fight their way out of a job.

With that sort of background it should not be wondered at if the best work the majority can find for themselves, when they are working, is some labouring job : this particular statistic does not prove that they are ineducable morons who (as one incensed reader recently wrote to a newspaper) ought to be sterilized before they bring any more unfortunate children into this world.

When I first began to investigate baby battering I expected to find many illegitimate babies among the victims. Unsupported mothers struggling against social disapproval, suffering economic hardship: the picture was an obvious one. In fact I was wrong; most battering is done inside a more or less stable family setting.

Let us look more closely at the kind of marital relationships battering parents have. Statistics can be misleading: Selwyn Smith found among his sample (1973) that almost one-third were unmarried and three-quarters of all the mothers had conceived before they married. However, the fact that a child is labelled illegitimate does not necessarily mean that the mother is not living with the father or with another man in a fairly stable relationship. The NSPCC *Retrospective Study* found that of their sample of 78 families, the majority (77 per cent) of the battered children were at the time of injury living with their natural parents, of whom fifty-four were married and only six unmarried. Another 18 per cent lived with their natural mother but with a substitute father (half of these couples were married to each other). Of the remaining four children there were only two living in single parent families, and in both these cases the parent was married but living apart from the spouse. A survey conducted by the National Opinion Research Center of the University of Chicago in 1965 found that over 80 per cent of the abused children in their survey lived with married parents or parent substitutes, and only 15 per cent were living with a single parent. Another survey carried out in New York City in 1966 by Simon and Downs found that only 2·4 per cent were one-parent families. They found, however, that 32 per cent of the children were legally illegitimate, as against the normal New York City average of 12 per cent. From all these figures it does seem that a higher than average number of battered children are conceived out of wedlock, but that the great majority live in a two-parent family, most often with both their natural parents.

Nevertheless, marriage or cohabitation does not necessarily prevent loneliness. Nowadays there is very little inter-family support, however large the wider family unit is: couples are expected to manage on their own without popping round to

Mum every few minutes, and there are few spinster aunts left in this modern world. Marriages are supposed to be self-sufficient in a way that has never happened before, and for some the strain is too great.

One of the problems is that these parents tend to pick each other out with unerring aim. Although many of these marriages follow on pre-marital conception and might therefore be considered unplanned, it takes two careless adults to make a baby : thoughtful responsible young men and women are not very likely to conceive an unwanted child. Experts on marriage sometimes remark how extraordinarily clever most people are at picking out either their opposites or their twins : they either marry someone they want to fight (perhaps continuing battles unsolved in their childhood) or they choose someone just like themselves. Some even manage to find a combination of the two, selecting a partner with similar emotional hang-ups to their own but with the basic characteristics of whichever parent they struggled most fiercely against. While such a situation can be therapeutic, the main danger is that when the battle is finished one spouse may emerge a changed character with no further need of the old partner.

Battering parents marry for the same reasons as everybody else, but the demands they make on marriage are excessive. They have a great need for reassurance, deep love, tenderness, strength : but neither side is capable of giving the other such gifts. Since they rarely believe in the value of words they cannot communicate with each other. Their demand is mute, and doomed to dissatisfaction. They want to receive love, but can only offer in exchange criticism and complaint.

The birth of a child complicates matters for the marriage partners even further. The love they did not succeed in wresting from their spouse they now hope to receive from their infant, but the new baby, instead of releasing in the mother the instant maternal love she had hoped to experience, merely produces exasperation and anger. In addition, if the father gives the baby the love and concern his wife feels he has denied her she will then be intolerably jealous, convinced not only that the baby

hates her (mistaking its cries of hunger or boredom for disapproval) but that it is also stealing her mate's love. The father,
who a few hours earlier may have been suffering exactly the
same emotion himself, may now take advantage of his temporary primacy and taunt the mother, suggesting that the baby
prefers him, or that she doesn't know how to look after it and
had better leave it to him. The situation is liable to see-saw,
each parent changing position, until the sense of strain in the
home grows to a dangerous intensity.

Such parents do not support each other, though support is
what they desperately need. They each sense the other's lacks
and despise them because they are their own lacks: at good
times they would reach out to the other but they cannot express themselves, and worst of all, they mistrust. However, their
very needs and fears bind them together in a hopeless struggle.

Where one of the parents is of the aggressive type the other
may be frightened to protect a child who is being attacked for
fear of drawing the violence to herself, though often such
people seem to invite the violence in subtle ways. (I am obviously not discussing here such problems as wife battering,
where the aggressiveness of the spouse is of another order
altogether.) Indeed, it is often impossible for investigators to
sort out who was responsible for any particular incident: collusion between the two parents can sometimes be so involved
that many feel there is no point in trying to discover who is the
'guilty' partner. Of course this pattern is not invariable: there
are marriages where one person is genuinely uninvolved, for
example through absence, but where two people are living together it is virtually impossible for one of them to have no idea
at all of how the other is treating their child.

Some research is being done on the kind of marriages battering parents have, but there are few facts available as yet. One
useful guideline to the recognition of a potentially dangerous
marriage has been outlined by Schneider, Pollock and Helfer
(1972) who suggest that there are basically three possibilities
where a person has had the kind of upbringing which could
result in his battering a child: the first is that if his potential to

batter is weak and he marries someone with a normal up-bringing he is unlikely to abuse his child; the second is that if his potential is strong and the spouse has a passive character, then almost certainly there will be abuse; lastly, if two adults with weak or moderate potentials marry, then battering is likely to occur. Obviously, if two people with strong potentials marry, then battering is almost certain to occur.

The lives of a married couple are so interwoven that disentangling the truth of it may be impossible in an ordinary social welfare situation: the marital problems can only be taken note of and the battering itself treated as the result of a family situation. If the situation continues to be explosive then the child should be removed until matters are mended; insisting on trying to find out which of the two partners actually committed a particular assault, or whether the partner who goaded the other into the attack was more to blame than the attacker, is not only pointless but actually harmful. The parents will be feeling guilty enough as it is without outsiders stirring up further rounds of accusations and arguments. Of course if the assault is a serious one and the law is involved then a social worker may have no choice in the matter. Either way, both parents must be talked to: taking the word of one parent only may lead to a misunderstanding of the reality of the marital situation.

Do battering parents see their children differently from the rest of us? How do they react to their babies, and why, if they love them so much, do they also attack them so cruelly? These vital questions are only just beginning to be answered, and various clues are emerging. Finding out the parent's genuine attitude to his child is complicated by the fact that he often does not know it himself. A child psychiatrist said, 'The early period of motherhood is universally accompanied by feelings of rage and anger. One's arrived at a situation in life where one has made a balance, one has one's pleasures, one's difficulties, but it's all organized, under control. Then suddenly there's this new life, everything's turned upside down, and it makes people angry, however much they want the child. You daren't allow these rejecting feelings near the surface, so you cope with them by being over-fussy, over-protective. One longs to say to such parents, for God's sake let him fall, let him scratch himself, he'll never learn otherwise. It's normal, it's the way most people are. Then most parents suddenly discover that children are tougher than they think and if they leave them for ten minutes nothing terrible will happen. A lot of parents don't discover this, however: they won't let go. It's the reverse of battering, you see, in a way, and yet it's the same process at work. It can end in battering, of course.'

Along with this over-cautious attitude there may be a physical distaste for the child resulting from the extreme disappointment the mother feels in it; although actually cuddling the child because she knows intellectually it needs such attention, the mother may nevertheless be hating the bodily contact. One mother said, 'I have to force myself to touch him; I'll pull him on to my lap by his clothes so that I don't actually have to get hold of him.' Imagine the turmoil in the mind of this mother who all through pregnancy longed to love and hold her own baby, only to find the reality repulsive and entirely unrewarding.

In Chapter 2 we showed how battering parents make excessive demands of their children, expect them to provide the parents with emotional support instead of the other way round. Their expectations are completely unreal, and are always far in advance of the capability of any child in a particular age group. Perhaps this mother had expected the baby to smile at her within a day or two of birth, to respond lovingly, to show immediately it knew who she was and perhaps to express some bond, some promise of a future loving relationship. This may sound ludicrous, but some of these desires are present in all mothers, and a baby's first open response to some caretaking action is a very precious moment. An unrealistic mother will be dissatisfied with the series of grunts and grimaces a new baby makes, will not find them enchanting and touching, but instead will see them as anger expressed against herself for somehow having failed. Her feelings for the baby will then be very ambivalent.

The widely-reported experiments with monkeys which had been reared by various surrogate mothers suggested that proper mothering of the future parent is essential if its eventual off-spring are themselves to be successfully mothered. How much one can make of these experiments with regard to human beings is a subject of debate; also one must bear in mind that these monkeys had to endure other unusual conditions besides unnatural mothering, such as a lack of their peers to play with, and these factors must also have had a bearing on the eventual sociability of the mother-to-be. However, commonsense would indicate that the results bear some relation to human mothers, especially when the findings are so similar to those reported by many researchers in the baby battering field. When the time came for the monkey mothers who had been deprived of normal mothering in their infancy to rear their own babies they pushed them aside, assaulted them, and even occasionally killed them. Aggression towards infants is not limited to the human species.

A psychiatrist suggested that it is not the fact that battering parents have these aggressive feelings which is important – all parents have them, he says – what matters is what they do with these feelings. If they have not learned to cope with them during childhood (and this is where learning how to get on with one's peers may possibly have as important an effect on the future adult – monkey or human – as poor mothering) then obviously difficulties will be experienced. Some of the origins of the aggression battering parents feel were discussed in Chapter 2; as to whether aggression is an inherent human trait or whether it is acquired is still debated. The psychiatrist Anthony Storr, who regards it as a natural drive and considers its proper understanding to be of fundamental importance to mankind, writes:

If we are to control aggression, it is important to determine whether there is . . . an internal accumulation of aggressive tension which needs periodic discharge, or whether the aggressive response is simply a potential which need never be brought into use. If the first supposition is true, what is needed to control aggression is the provision of suitable outlets for aggression. If the latter is true, what is required is the avoidance of all stimuli which might arouse the aggressive response.

Whichever is true, the outcome for many battering mothers is the same: the only *outlet* in such a housebound mother's life may be her family, and unfortunately the response is normally such that the aggression is intensified, and not worked out. As to avoiding all stimuli, few situations could be more stimulating for a potential aggressor than an unresponsive, demanding baby lying screaming for attention while the spouse is out at a football match or sitting with hands over ears reading a magazine.

The attack, when it does come, may well pass right out of the attacker's mind immediately afterwards, so that he or she will be unable to recall what happened. Cameron writes that 'guilt-amnesia is a well-recognized condition in most of the abusive parents': certainly the parent is likely to be extremely hazy about what actually happened, owing to the emotional turmoil taking place in his mind at the time. The child may be momentarily seen as the attacker's parent, or as himself as a child, or as some hateful amalgam of everything the attacker detests about himself and others. The picture left in the attacker's mind after the assault may be so confused and unreal he is genuinely quite unable to make any sense of it or to relate the thing he attacked to his own familiar child. Some parents, however, are able to recall clearly enough what happened, but will lie because of fear of the consequences, or from straightforward guilt. It is a rare parent who can bring himself to openly admit what took place.

Finally, what makes some parents attack their own children, while others are able to overcome their impulses? That some mothers suffering from puerperal or post-natal depression 'lose their minds' and kill their young babies has been accepted for some time now with understanding. Such a mother usually receives sympathy and will not be imprisoned. The emotive term 'battering' is not normally used in such cases of infanticide, although it may well be that some of these babies had earlier on suffered undetected abuse. Why should the young mother suffering from post-natal depression, who is found to have assaulted her child, not be treated with the same sympathy as one who actually kills it? I cannot help feeling that there may be an artificial distinction between these two categories based on the abhorrence of the idea that a mother could kill her own child and the intense need of everyone concerned to find a valid explanation. Puerperal depression is a perfect excuse, can be seen as an illness and is therefore forgivable. One imagines the mother in a sudden access of anguish cleanly killing her baby. But in fact these children die by stabbing, strangling, smothering, drowning and bashing: where then is the difference? If hormonal disturbances are at the bottom of the mother's depression, this will affect millions of mothers. Might one therefore not expect there to be large numbers of mild cases of bashing where the disturbance is comparatively mild? Does a severe hormonal disturbance normally result in one sudden violent attack causing immediate death, or is the killing perhaps the result of progressive bashing which has remained unrecognized, as in many ordinary cases of baby battering?

Kempe and Helfer (1972) suggest that one of the causes of postnatal depression may be that some mothers are distressed because they find they cannot love their babies, the more usual theory being the reverse, that they could not love their babies because they were suffering from depression brought on by the pregnancy and birth itself. Whatever the cause for puerperal depression, it is an important factor to be reckoned with. Most workers in contact with young mothers know of its effect, and several told me they were certain it was behind many of the attacks their mothers had made. Skinner and Castle (1969) state that of the forty adult mothers in their sample seventeen were pregnant at the time of the battering incident and another four had battered an older child within two months of giving birth to a new baby: that is, 52 per cent were either recently confined or were pregnant at the time they made their attack. Similarly-based figures are not given for the 1972 report, but out of 292 children, 56 were under five months old and a further 54 were between six and eleven months old, that is to say, over a third of the children were under eleven months old when they were attacked, falling within the age limit for infanticide. How many mothers were pregnant again at the time of the attack is unknown, but a certain number were bound to have been. Here is another field where further research is badly needed.

Premature birth brings problems of its own. For a start, the mother is completely separated from the child at birth, preventing the normal process of imprinting where permanent impressions of the other are made on each partner. If this process is most effective immediately after birth, a separation perhaps lasting two or three months may prevent a satisfactory imprint being achieved. The mother may find it impossible to feel any physical or emotional connection with the tiny raw-looking baby lying sealed away from her in its hygienic cot, side by side with a dozen other such babies. She may be upset by its appearance, even revolted by it, and by the time the child is returned to her she may feel it is a total stranger.

The NSPCC found in their 1969 and 1972 samples that 13 to 14 per cent of the assaulted children were classified as premature, a classification which includes those children who are born in the normal time span but are underweight at birth and therefore need special treatment. This figure is double that of the national average. The question to be solved here is how interlinked are these facts? Were the babies premature or underweight because of stresses in the pregnant mother, or was it the failure to have a normal birth and the problems arising from prematurity which upset the mother *after* birth, causing the stress which later resulted in battering? The 1969 *Retrospective Study* reports that the premature babies, along with a further group of failure-to-thrive babies, were rather more severely injured than other normal babies. Certainly a weakly baby needing extra care is not the best kind of infant for a mother with a battering potential to rear.

It appears that some babies are more likely to be attacked than others. Premature and underweight babies are automatically in danger. Not only does their care demand extra patience on the part of both parents, but the mere fact that they are 'difficult', with its implication that the parents have not been able to achieve a normal baby, will be enough to rouse antagonism in anyone with a battering potential. A baby who does not eat well, or who wakes up full of energy in the middle of the night will also cause much stress. Many babies have different body rhythms from their parents, or have body clocks functioning outside the twenty-four-hour cycle so that it is unusually difficult to train them to fit into a normal time pattern. Even well-adjusted parents can find this situation almost intolerable.

If the parent has only a weak impulse to batter and he is blessed with a contented baby which sleeps most of the day and all the night, which obligingly eats all it is given and puts on the right amount of weight, all is likely to be well. If, however, the baby is not quite perfect in some way, perhaps has a small birth mark or some other defect, or if he suffers from three-month colic or is very fussy with his food, then he is in some danger, especially with a parent whose potential is fairly strong.

When the mother was pregnant she no doubt fantasized about her future child. Perhaps she desperately wanted a girl and dreaded having a boy. If when the child is born it turns out to be a male, then the chances are already stacked against him. Equally many men long for a son, and will be bitterly disappointed if a girl is born. If the baby reminds a potentially dangerous parent of some member of the family (including him- or herself) about whom he has strongly unhappy feelings then the child is in danger. A good question for social workers or doctors to ask such parents is whether the baby looks like or behaves like anyone in the family. If the reply is 'Yes, he's got my husband's temper', or 'She's got all my faults, I'm afraid', then they should sit up and take notice.

An important symptom is that the child is often seen by the parents to be different from other children, although the worker may be quite unable to spot any such difference. The idea that one particular child may be chosen as a scapegoat was popular for some time, and while this situation certainly does exist, it is probably a separate problem from the battered baby syndrome. A true scapegoated child may be locked away, starved, beaten, denied light and fresh air, while all the other children in the family are brought up quite normally. With battered children the distinction between the children is rarely so clear-cut. There may be one particular child which is being beaten at the moment, and because such parents are often extremely fussy about clothing and general caretaking the other children may seem to have escaped all abuse. However, in many such cases on looking up old medical records it has been found that the siblings have also suffered a series of 'accidents' in their time.

Few statistics are available at present to prove how likely a parent is to batter all of his children or only one of them, but some were put forward in the NSPCC's 1969 *Retrospective Study*. The sample of 78 families was too small to be totally inclusive : for instance, there was only one family with as many as four children in it (most of the families in the study were still young and therefore not yet very prolific). However, 68 per cent of the families for which complete details were obtained had battered their first-born child. More may have done so, but no hospitalization was recorded for the rest. In the 22 families where the first-born was battered and further children had been born, 26 out of the 28 siblings were also battered. The authors tentatively estimate that any second children born in the eighteen families which up to then had only had one child stood a 13 to 1 chance of being battered. These figures are based on a small number of cases, and incomplete data were available. A much wider survey including some bigger families with older supposedly-untouched children who could be X-rayed for healed fractures, etc., would be invaluable. For the time being one may perhaps assume that if a parent's battering potential is not very strong and if circumstances do not go too severely against him or her, then it may be that only one child will receive any battering severe enough to need some form of medical treatment. But if unfortunate crises occur, or if the battering potential is strong, then all the children in the family will be in danger. Certainly where the first child has been battered every subsequent child should be considered as being at risk also.

The power of a child's cry is phenomenal. Watch what happens in any shopping street full of housewives if a child yells 'Mum!' Heads of young mothers, middle-aged women and even grandmothers turn instinctively, immediately, searching out the crier. Once you have been a mother your child may be grown up and in another country, but if such a cry sounds urgent, perhaps signifying danger, for a moment the old feelings are awoken and adrenalin starts pumping through you before you have a chance to smile at your mistake. A persistently crying child can break down concentration or peace of mind quicker than any other noise known to man. There was a post-war story that tapes of crying babies used to be played outside the bunkers of stubborn Japanese soldiers who refused to capitulate. Within a short time they invariably came running out, begging for the tapes to be stopped. It could have been true : it almost certainly would have worked.

In the next and final chapter we will look at the story of a girl whose child nearly drove her to battering because night after night it woke crying, sometimes several times a night, until she was almost beside herself with fatigue and anger. Let anyone who still says, 'I just can't understand how any parent can bring themselves to hit a child in anger', read this story and put himself in the place of the mother. She survived the experience and the baby came out of it unscathed, but they were lucky. Many parents and babies aren't.

Chapter 9

What can be done to help?

Susan Parkinson is a tall heavily-built girl who looks you straight in the eye and whose handgrasp is so overpowering you need to rub your knuckles for a minute or two before they cease aching. I first met her at a party when she overheard me talking about this book. She came up to me afterwards and without any apparent embarrassment said, 'I used to batter my children. Would you like me to tell you about it?' We agreed to meet several days later, but I did not really expect her to turn up. I had misjudged her, however. She was already waiting for me, obviously impatient to begin.

'I exaggerated the other night, I didn't really batter my kids, not what a court would call battering, anyway. But I came near enough. I've been thinking about it all since I spoke to you, and a lot of things have got clearer.

'The main trouble was that my daughter had this crazy sleep pattern that didn't fit in with anybody else's. She'd stay awake all night and only sleep properly in the morning. Oh, she'd doze for an hour or two, but then she'd wake up again and that would go on all through the night. It was all right at the beginning because she'd go back to sleep again after a few minutes. It really doesn't disturb me at all to have to potter around at night occasionally, not the way it would some people – I didn't even mind getting up three or four times a night, as long as once I'd kissed her and tucked her up I could get back to bed. But when she was about four months old she changed. She began to stay awake, got very active and demanding, and no matter how quietly I crept out she'd know, and start bawling for me.

'When I look back now I see I was absolutely crazy not to take her into my room with me. Why didn't I? Because of my husband. He's insensible at night, totally saturated with sleep, and if something wakes him up his first reaction is rage. I suppose I should have insisted, but there were a lot of reasons. . . . For one thing, he hadn't wanted children in the first place. We're both musicians; he's a flautist and whenever he has a concert he works himself up to a state even if he's only playing in the orchestra. He can't help it, it's his way. And musicians need to be free to travel, whereas children are bound to tie you down. I'm a singer and I can't say having children has exactly helped my career. I'm taking it up again now, but it's uphill work, once you've dropped out. But let's be quite clear about it; I wanted kids, and I'm very glad I had them. I love them, I get a great deal of pleasure from them: don't think I don't just because I nearly bashed the daylights out of them.

'I went ahead and had a baby in spite of my husband, and at first he was mad. Then he accepted it. He'd had a lousy childhood himself and for him a nice jolly family group just wasn't on. It wasn't a real possibility. In fact he's very fond of the kids now, he's better with them than I am sometimes. But you see I felt I couldn't wake him up, make him take his turn, not when I'd foisted her onto him like that. So every time she woke I'd creep out of the room as silently as I could so as not to wake him.

'The room she slept in was another mistake. We were mad, looking back on it. We'd bought a delapidated old house that was falling down, all we could afford at the time, but it had lots of rooms and a big garden, perfect for kids. It was in a terrible state, though; the previous owner had let out all the rooms individually and they stank of other people's stale cooking fat and dirty washing – awful! Because she was only a baby, we thought she wouldn't notice such things, so we didn't rush to do her room up. The walls were stained with damp and when we pulled the paper off to see what the plaster was like underneath greats lumps of it fell away so you could see the bare laths in places. We'd taken up the lino because it was worn out and a terrible design: as a result the floor boards creaked every time you crossed the floor and there was a dreadful draught. We had no central heating then, nothing fancy like that, so you can imagine how freezing it was at night. It was a *horrible* room, sordid and foul. And we expected a baby to sleep in that! Mind you, the rest of the house was the same, but *we* knew what we were doing it all for, she didn't.

'When I first brought her home I was nearly in a state of panic. I wasn't really prepared for the shock of having a baby. I remember bringing her into the house (we'd only moved in a few months before and were in the middle of disembowelling the place) and being quite appalled at what I'd done. Having this small thing so dependent on you! The house seemed too disgusting to bring a child into, but outside it was worse. At first I couldn't bring myself to expose her to all those traffic fumes or the noise. I couldn't ever leave her outside shops, not ever. I suppose I was overprotective; it's not that I want to protect them from experience, I don't, but there are some things I can't endure exposing them to. I suppose I'm very suspicious of the outside world really.

'I sat looking at her, and I thought, without me this creature will die. It depends entirely on me for its life. I was no longer a single person at all – I was living a dual life now and would for ever, totally. The bashing had its origins right there, I suppose, because I couldn't be cool enough about being a mother. But I couldn't help it: I sat looking at her and I was *overwhelmed* by the responsibility I'd taken on. I couldn't cut off from her, it was as though we were still physically connected. For instance, I'd wake up when she did. I'd lie there knowing she had woken and would start crying at any moment, and sure enough the cry always came, sometimes immediately, sometimes not for several minutes. The moment she cried, almost before I heard the sound, I'd be out of bed, the adrenalin going *whoosh* through my whole body.

'I'd have this great physical response, my whole body was sweating and prickling afterwards. I could have taken on a tiger, fought off an army, I had so much sheer bodily strength because of the sound of her cry, and instead I had to pick up this ridiculously tiny child and soothe it. Physically I was prepared for something much more immense, do you see? Then I had to sit there beside her, getting colder and colder in that ghastly room, and knowing that hours of cold lay ahead of me. I'd walk up and down with her in my arms, or sing to her, or tickle her or shout at her or any damn thing to try to send her off. But nothing would. I might be there one hour, two hours. Then I'd get away, sleep for a bit, and there'd she be calling again. Four or five times a night, most nights. Until six or seven in the morning. Then she'd fall asleep and sleep until ten like a rock.

'It was when we began to get a bit more settled that I first attacked her. Her bedroom was beginning to look more like a nursery and things were easing up, so I suppose I felt why can't the bloody baby ease up too? She must have been about a year old before I started getting really desperate. I'd be in such a state by the fourth or fifth time she woke me. My dreams were endlessly interrupted. I'd stand there trembling, not able to take it any more. Shaking her was the first thing I did. I'd grip her, grip her like this, but in a way I wasn't so much holding her tight as holding myself. My muscles would go absolutely tense, rigid, then I'd make a funny sort of grunting noise from breathing out suddenly after I'd been holding my breath. At first I didn't hurt her at all. But later I'd shake her, shake her really hard, or pick her up and throw her down in the cot so violently she'd bounce up again. Perhaps she'd be sitting up and I'd give her a shove, push her down yelling "*lie down*, you bloody awful child!"

'No, I never banged her head or anything. I always took great care not to really hurt her. I frequently cracked her head carrying her through doors, though, but that was unintentional, just me being clumsy. I never drew blood or bruised either of them through an action of mine or marked them in any way. The most I've done is to make them cry uncontrollably, and once they were doing that, I'd calm down. I used to throw them to the floor too, but only so they'd land on their nappy. They never got hurt.

'The funny thing is the one I attacked most dangerously was my second daughter, and yet she was much less trouble to me than the first. She's always been a cheerful easy little thing. I only attacked her once like that, when she was about two and a half, but I really did almost lose my mind that time. She'd been playing a game but I had to interrupt her because we were going out. It was a freezing cold day and I had to bundle her up into masses of clothes. But every time I got something onto her she ripped it off again, because she wanted to go back to playing her game. In the end I lost my temper and I *belaboured* her. In fact I'd dressed her by then, but she started to pull off her coat again, screaming at me. I shoved her down on the floor and I hit her and hit her and hit her. I knew I wasn't hurting her very much because she was so thickly covered with clothes it was like beating a cushion. I think too I was so tense that a lot of my energy was going into stiffening up my muscles rather than hitting her. A friend's child was there as well as my other daughter, and they both kept shouting, "Stop it! Stop it!" So I did stop, and I picked her up by the neck, pulling her straight up as though she were a heavy puppy. Then suddenly I was utterly horrified with myself. I wanted to break her neck, because I felt so sorry for her. That's daft, isn't it, but I knew I was spoiling things for her and I thought, why should I have the right to interrupt her pleasures just because I'm bigger than she is? But she was resisting me, and I thought she might at least be polite about it, like I had been trying to be. God knows what exactly my feelings were then, but I know I felt very sympathetic towards her, I understood her rejecting me but her rejection was making things desperately awkward, so I felt like breaking her neck. Yet I'd never been angry with her before, apart from the passing annoyances any toddler causes.

'I've never hit either of them again like that. I scared myself, I suppose. I've pushed them so that they'd fall down – I intended them to fall down – but most of it was mock fury. With children it's often like that, they attack you physically and it's half a mock attack, and sometimes it turns into a rough and tumble, sometimes it can enrage you. I've given them a tremendous kick and sent them hurtling across the room with my foot. But I'm physically violent anyway, physically demonstrative, physically active, and I use my hands to express everything. I smack them quickly, slap them hard, but none of it's out of control. It's a momentary fury and it's more animal than anything else. I react quickly, roughly, like an animal, but it doesn't mean anything bad. The children know that, they entirely accept it. They know how I react; I once hit a complete stranger in a train, so hitting my own kids is no great step for me. But I've never thrown them so that they'd hit their heads against a wall or done something to really endanger them.

'You know, thinking about being an animal: that's just how it was. I'd wake up in the night – I still do it, even now – and I'd sniff the air. I'd lie rigid, listening, every sense awake, listening for danger. Sedatives? Yes, the doctor gave me bottles and bottles for her, and when it didn't work he'd tell me to double the dose, so I'd try that and still it didn't work. She'd go to sleep all right, but she'd soon wake up. Nothing ever stopped her waking up.

'She still does, but it doesn't matter now. Sometimes she wanders around on her own, or she calls me and I go in and give her a quick cuddle and she lets me go again. My other daughter does the same, but afterwards I go straight back to sleep; even if it happens several times in a night it doesn't worry me. It was only when she wouldn't let me go, when I had to stand there freezing hour after hour, knowing that even when I got back to bed it would only be a short time before it started all over again.

'Once I tried ignoring the call. I lay there, so miserable it was terrible. It's the worst nightmare I can imagine, calling in the dark, and no one comes. I never did it again; it seems to me so much worse than bashing her, to leave her crying alone. Why do I feel that? I don't know, I'm sure I wasn't left as a child, not as a baby, anyway. My mother was a marvellous woman, very tender and careful of our feelings. She never intruded, was always very polite to us, never pushed her own feelings onto us. Yes, I suppose it's true, she was a bit cold to us, but it was only me that felt it. I always had this animal thing about touching, and I think she found it a bit embarrassing, you know? My sister was very like her emotionally, and I remember once, when

I was about twelve and my sister was fourteen, that she was very cross with me because I was cuddling my mother, making a fuss of her. And my mother was very wise, she explained to my sister that it was my nature to be like that, that I was impulsive and needed to touch people, and she should accept the difference and try to understand it. No, I don't think my mother liked cuddling, or at least, she certainly didn't hug and play with us the way I do my own children, but she was a marvellous mother, much better than ever I could be. She had such respect for everybody, that she couldn't have mauled us around in the crude way I do mine. She thought you should treat children with the same respect you do adults. Perhaps she was too cool, I don't know. I've never really looked at it like that. Perhaps as a result I felt a bit ashamed of being the sort of bear I am. But it wasn't any doing of hers, she was a wonderful woman, everybody who knew her loved her. It was just me. I must have been a difficult child in many ways. I used to wake up at night too, I believe, and I know when I was older I used to get up and wander around the house just the way my two do. It's hereditary I suppose, and there's nothing much you can do about it. Sedatives are just a waste of time, and I'm sure it can't do a child any good, to keep thrusting medicine down its throat just because it can't sleep when *you* happen to want it to. Maybe I should have taken the sedative instead.'

The family whose story has just been described and Maria Colwell's family live such different lives that few points of resemblance can be found between them. Yet in both a parent attacked a child. Susan Parkinson never completely lost control, however, and no one reading her story can feel other than pity and sympathy for her. But it is not so easy to feel pity for William Kepple.

The Government inquiry concerning Maria Colwell received so much press coverage that most people will be familiar with the outline of the case. On 6 January 1973 William Kepple came home drunk late in the evening, found Maria, his step-daughter, sitting watching television, and beat her savagely. The following morning he and his wife wheeled her to hospital, where she was found to be dead. The step-father was sentenced to life imprisonment for murder, but on appeal this was reduced to eight years for manslaughter. Complaints that Maria's case had not been handled properly resulted later in the year in a Government inquiry lasting nine weeks, during which every aspect of Maria's case was examined.

The whole story of Maria proves the urgency of the various suggestions made in this book. Lack of cooperation between the various bodies concerned, vital information not passed on to the proper quarters, the lack of recognition of the battering syndrome by doctors and others; all these typical points of failure are horrifyingly illustrated by Maria's case. Aged seven she falls outside the currently accepted age limits for baby battering, but in many other ways she fits into the known battering pattern. I will give only a brief résumé of the case : lack of space prevents me from describing the whole story which is more complicated than these few pages will show. Nor is there space for the excuses which no doubt could be made for the various workers involved, though these may be deduced from my earlier chapters. Meanwhile, the inescapable fact remains that Maria was killed, as many people feared she would be.

Maria's father died when she was four and a half months old. The mother's care of her children was so poor that within three months of his death the NSPCC was forced to separate Maria and her four siblings from her and put them into different foster homes. Maria was taken in by her dead father's sister, Mrs Cooper, who eventually became her legal foster mother under a care order which gave parental rights to East Sussex County Council. From then on Maria's life was a happy one, and she grew into a healthy, happy little girl. However, when she was six years old her natural mother, now married to William Kepple (by whom she had had a further three children) decided she wanted her daughter back home. Mrs Cooper desperately tried to prevent the separation, but Mrs Kepple managed to persuade Miss Lees, the County Council child care officer, that Maria's best interests would be served by giving her back to her natural mother. Miss Lees later said, 'Even when a child expresses difficulty about seeing a parent, I still feel there is a feeling about the natural parent. I agree it is current thinking and it is supported by my experience.'

Maria was sent to her mother for trial weekends, hated them, and had to be dragged away from her foster mother screaming and crying. She returned from the weekends dirty and very unhappy, and began to wet her bed. The family GP found that Maria was suffering from depression. Nevertheless, in November 1971 the care order giving East Sussex County Council parental rights over Maria was revoked, and Mrs Kepple resumed control over her daughter. The court made a supervision order for the social services in Brighton to keep an eye on Maria's progress, but in order to keep up the continuity Miss Lees was retained as the child care officer responsible for supervising her. No one at the court hearing thought it necessary to ask Maria her opinion, or to contact or even to inform the legal foster mother about the vital decision being made. There was no investigation into Mr and Mrs Kepple's style of life, and the fact that Kepple had had four convictions for brawling and common assault was not brought up.

From then on Maria's life rapidly deteriorated. Between April and December 1972 there were thirty complaints about Maria to various welfare agencies and fifty-six official visits were made to the house, though Maria herself was rarely seen. Her teacher, who said, 'I shuddered when I felt how thin she was. She was like a bird and I was frightened of crushing her', made frequent complaints to her headmaster; as a result the education welfare officer visited the Kepples' house seventeen times between July and December. The Kepples' however, were very successful at keeping Maria out of sight, and she only managed to see her once. Miss Lees, the child care officer, failed to see Maria at all between June and December 1972, although the child was under her supervision. Various neighbours rang the police and the NSPCC, complaining that the children were left unattended at night while both parents were out drinking, and that Maria had been seen at a window with 'her face terribly blackened and one eye was a pool of blood'. They stated at the inquiry that it had been obvious the child was starving, and indeed at her death she was found to weigh 36 lb, only two-thirds the normal weight for a seven-year-old child.

The police were called for a variety of reasons to the Kepples' home, and Brighton's housing officer was even asked by neighbours to remove the family from their council house because of the parents' drunkenness and obscene language, and because the children defecated on the pavement. Meanwhile, during the last term at school, the rumour spread among the other children that Maria was beaten at home and locked up in a cupboard. She continued to be late for school because she had first to fetch shopping, including heavy bags of coal. She must have made some protest: at the inquiry Maria's step-sister said that her mother had taken the handle away from the child's bedroom door to prevent her running away, though Mrs Kepple later denied this.

Pressure from the school welfare officer and the NSPCC resulted in an appointment being made for Maria at the Brighton school clinic, and on her card was written: 'Neglect has been reported in this case, and some battery. The child has appeared bruised. Urgent appointment made.' But Mrs Kepple broke the appointment, and due to an administrative error the card was filed away and no new appointment was made. A doctor who did see Maria on 6 December at his surgery for a scalp rash, sore throat, abdominal pains and diarrhoea suspected nothing, however, in spite of two red marks on her cheekbones and her light weight. Had he known of the general concern about her, he said at the inquiry, he would have read these signs very differently.

Finally, on 1 December, after a gap of five and a half months, Miss Lees managed to see Maria for herself. Although the girl had lost 'a tremendous amount of weight' the social worker felt all was well. She saw Maria for the last time on 13 December and felt satisfied that she was settling down at last, although in fact Maria had not been to school since 18 November and was never to go again.

On 6 January Maria was killed. Dr James Cameron said, 'In all my experience I have never seen a worse case of bruising. There was virtually no part of the body free from staining by bruises.' He also found a previously fractured rib, undoubtedly the result of an earlier attack, which would have shown up on X-rays if anyone had ever thought fit to submit the still living child to such an examination.

I have chosen to finish this book with these two illustrations – Susan Parkinson, who never caused a real injury, and William Kepple, who killed, because they represent the two extremes of battering. Our society completely failed to help these two families, and a child's death was the result in one case. What alterations to the present inadequate system must be made if future tragedies are to be avoided?

Let us look at the Parkinsons, because they needed comparatively little assistance, and because there are many thousands of parents like them. Some do not hit as hard as Susan did, others hit harder. Some have less luck when they boot their children across the room or crack their babies' heads as they pass through doorways, ending up with hospitalized children. When I showed a social worker Susan's story she exclaimed, 'It's so typical! I could show you a dozen similar cases on my patch alone.' We look after the physical health of our pregnant mothers and later their new born babies very carefully, but we completely ignore their emotional and mental health.

I am not suggesting analysis for every new mother and psychiatric tests for all young children, but something much simpler which would cost very little to organize. We already have a system of pre-natal and post-natal clinics which the majority of mothers attend. Why should not the post-natal clinics run a weekly new mothers' club to which all first-time mothers automatically go? A group of local experienced mothers could help by acting as non-professional guides to the exhilarating but exhausting career of motherhood, and also perhaps by brewing up pots of tea in a room adjoining the clinic. When the new babies have had their weight checked and other routine jobs are completed, their mothers, the nurses, midwife, clinic doctor, social worker and anyone else involved in the clinic could join in a general discussion over tea and biscuits.

Most new mothers are desperate for information, for reassurance that their baby will survive now it is exposed to ordinary home life and no longer in the baby ward at the hospital. I remember hardly daring to shut my eyes the first night I brought my baby home in case it choked or suffocated; never before had it slept without a night nurse in attendance, while by day its weight and progress had been continuously checked by a series of experts. Now there was no one but me to recognize any terrible illness it might at that very moment be developing. Looking back, and realizing how much I have learned about bringing up children since then, I realize I was quite right to be frightened! I was appallingly ignorant of anything to do with children, and if it had not been for my sympathetic husband and my well-thumbed copy of Dr Spock, I don't know how I or my baby would have managed. Every new mother needs cosseting, and mother-centred gatherings such as I have suggested would be of inestimable value to those who unexpectedly find themselves nervous and uncertain of their capability of rearing a minute, frighteningly vulnerable infant.

Imagine then how useful such meetings would be to potential batterers among the new mothers. During the general talk one of the staff would need to ensure that feelings of aggression are adequately discussed: the experienced mothers could easily be primed to talk about and if necessary slightly exaggerate their own bad times. Since only a few new mothers would be present at any one meeting they might feel able to discuss any feelings of aggression towards and disappointment in their children which they had already experienced. If such feelings cannot be brought out into the open, at least a mother at risk will know she is not unique, that her feelings are universal even if she has them more strongly than most. Above all, she has learned that there will always be somewhere to go to if she needs help, a place where what she might otherwise have considered unmentionable may in fact be openly talked about. Obviously any mother expressing more than the usual amount of fear or aggression could be noted and her local health visitor asked to keep a special though tactful eye on her.

A second more direct way of helping new mothers with a battering potential would be the system of mothering aids already discussed. However, for some time to come such help would probably have to be reserved for cases where mild assaults had already taken place. Various methods of gathering together bands of such women ought to be considered urgently: if necessary, payment should be made. Psychiatrists charge patients a great deal for their expertise: why should not ordinary women willing to devote some of their time to the problems of others be given a small remuneration for their trouble?

Third, could not night nurseries be considered? For parents suffering from the 'crying child' syndrome, even an occasional free night would help preserve their sanity. However, since the Government will not at present provide sufficient day nurseries it is unlikely they would consider the possibility of night nurseries. Perhaps parents could get together and arrange some such system for themselves, just as many nowadays arrange play groups? Young babies can easily be carried around in carrycots, and older children would probably accept occasional nights with friends whom they already know. It would mean a bad night for the parents on duty, but they would have their free night to look forward to. Lists exhibited at local clinics could provide the original introduction of similarly-suffering parents, but this might involve the risk of leaving one's child with a potential batterer. Obviously it would be very unwise to begin night-swapping sessions until all the parents and children concerned had had the chance to get to know each other well during daytime meetings. Perhaps the social worker attached to the clinic ought to be in charge of any such lists so that she could check out the parents involved and satisfy herself as to their reliability.

Lastly, in America there has been formed a self-help group similar to Alcoholics Anonymous, called Mothers Anonymous.

Since 1970 the mothers of MA, as it is known, have helped each other to overcome their aggressive urges towards their children. Meeting regularly, they support each other through difficult times, apparently gaining a great deal of pleasure and satisfaction from being of use to others. In the past as individuals they found professioonal help of little use, and now as a group they still eschew such assistance. Kempe and Helfer, who describe the workings of MA in *Helping the Battered Child and his Family*, suggest, however, that the group has now reached the stage where they need professional help to aid them pass beyond the negative aim of not hitting their babies, to the more positive state of learning how to love and appreciate them.

A similar group could provide a very useful breakthrough in Britain. Certainly many doctors and organizations such as the NSPCC would be willing to give their assistance if it were asked for, and it would be a pity if it were not. Professional knowledge would be particularly useful in teaching patterns of normal child behaviour, thus helping the parents to adjust their ideas about what is realistic to expect from a child and what is not.

Such a group would probably not reach families like Maria Colwell's, however. In many families of this kind not even intensive social work care and constant supervision will be sufficient, and the question has to be asked as to whether or not a particular parent will ever be capable of looking after a child. Mrs Kepple, for example, had earlier shown herself unable to look after her five children and they had been removed from her care. Why then was Maria returned to her? Can it have been thought that her marriage to a man known for drunken assaults would help her to be a better mother? The social workers considered Maria's return to be inevitable, and therefore felt that the sooner it was over and done with the better. But *why* should her return have been inevitable?

It has to be accepted even by the juvenile courts that not every parent is a good parent, or is even a possible parent. Some children have to be removed from their homes, and once they have been removed very great care must be taken before they are returned. It ought to be impossible for any court to rescind a care order without investigating fully the natural parents' background, home life and mental stability. If a child is happy where he is he should not be taken away unless there is a very good reason for it.

As a result of the Maria Colwell case it has been suggested that Children's Advocates are needed. At present the parents' interests are almost invariably put before those of their children on the grounds that, blood being thicker than water, the children are bound to be happiest with their own parents in the long run, whatever their present desires. The Colwell case and many like it show this to be demonstrably untrue. And yet it is only parents who plead their case in court, assisted by state-financed lawyers : why should not their children be represented automatically by someone appointed to look after their sole interests? There should be no second-class citizens in a democracy, whether by reason of race, sex, religion or age.

If, in Maria's case, such an advocate had been able to plead her cause, it is possible the court would not have made the decision to return her to her mother. Or, at the very least, it might have ordered closer supervision to be kept upon her progress. As it was, she was returned to a highly unsuitable home, unwanted by a step-father who already had three children of his own, and who had a reputation for violence.

It might have been considered that so many people knew about Maria that it was impossible for her to fall through the social welfare net spread under her, but she did. How was this? For one thing, the child care officer under whose supervision she had been placed had a heavy case load of seventy, including six children considered to be at risk. The NSPCC knew about the Kepple family, but it was not the job of their officers to interfere with Miss Lees's arrangements when she was the officially appointed officer in charge of the case. The police had done all they could, having warned the parents against leaving the children unattended at night, but they had no further evidence to act upon. The educational officer was very worried about Maria and had decided to make further inquiries when the spring term started. But it was too late by then; Maria was already dead.

The only way in which further tragedies of this kind can be avoided in the future is by greatly improved coordination between all the professional bodies involved. Certain hospitals in America already employ team coordinators with great success. A coordinator's job is to follow the progress of specified clients, and to ensure that all knowledge concerning them is coordinated. She is the contact between parents and doctors, social workers and police. She sees that parents keep their appointments, tracks them down if they move away, and personally guides them through the sometimes confusing world of officialdom. Since she has no other duties, she has time to be patient with difficult clients and time to look up records; above all she is the only person to have a continuous up-to-date picture of the overall situation.

The combination of a Children's Advocate who should not only plead the child's interest in court but should also ensure that any child he considers at risk is put on a list of children to be supervised, and a Coordinator whose job it is to follow the progress of any child on such a list, should cast a safety net infinitely more reliable than the present moth-eaten one. If everyone involved in Maria's case had known what all the others knew individually, then most of them would have behaved differently. The doctor would no doubt have X-rayed Maria and discovered her cracked rib, the child care officer would have insisted on seeing Maria in person and finding out why she had not been at school, instead of accepting her mother's lies. Maria might even have been interviewed away from the intimidating presence of her parents and the real truth discovered from her own lips.

In America most coordinators are hospital-centred: probably in England they would have to be a part of the social services. An alternative would be to set up a central unit whose sole concern was child abuse, where coordinators would be trained before being sent out to different areas. The NSPCC has set up a National Advisory Centre on the Battered Child to replace their Battered Child Research Department. Their aims are to 'offer education and consultative services on a nationwide basis to all the professions concerned. Facilities available would include a well-equipped library, with current literature on the subject of battered children, video tapes, recordings and films. A full range of medical, psychological and psychiatric services would be provided to hospitals and the community.'

Such a centre will indeed be of great value. Its growth, however, depends on the funds allocated to it, and by its very nature the NSPCC is financially limited : surely it is up to the Government to finance such a project, and to do so quickly.

In addition to the services planned by the NSPCC's new centre, there ought somewhere to be a national list to which the name of every child known or suspected to be battered is added; such a service would have to be computerized and run with superb efficiency as information of this nature needs to be instantly available. Also, all research projects under way or in the process of preparation should be listed at such a national centre : at the moment half the people working in this field not only have no idea what the other half are doing, they also have no idea who they are. There is still so much to be found out, so many opposing views on the values of various treatments, that it is time order was brought to a chaotic situation.

The only way that this can be achieved is for an independent regularly-meeting national board to be formed at high level right across the various professions concerned – Directors of Social Services, the NSPCC, heads of police forces, doctors, psychiatrists, nurses, etc. – only then will the time-wasting and occasionally disastrous problems of cooperation be overcome. In 1973 a group of such people met in Tunbridge Wells to form a study group, during which the whole subject of baby battering was discussed. Many resolutions were passed, and it is to be hoped that positive action will follow. Such meetings ought to take place on a regular basis, and men and women at the highest professional level ought to consider it unthinkable that they or their representatives should not take part. Few of the many committee meetings which top-ranking people have to attend could affect the future of our children more profoundly or be of greater humantitarian importance.

The Maria Colwell case has brought child abuse to the fore-front of public attention. Questions are being asked in the House, changes in the law are being suggested. But change takes time, and the danger is that once public excitement has died down present pressure will be relaxed. This must not be allowed to happen. Seven hundred children are being killed every year and four or five thousand seriously battered, many of whom will suffer from the effects of brain damage all their lives. More than a few alterations to the law are needed : there has to be a change of attitude on the part of doctors, social service workers, the police, and every one of us.

Between the millions of parents who sometimes feel exasper-ated and only just manage to refrain from striking their child, and the comparative few who batter to the point of death, there is an unbroken ladder. It is our job to learn how to pluck parents from that ladder before they have progressed very far up it. To do that we need knowledge, money to finance the acquisition of that knowledge, endless compassion and understanding. Is that too much to ask of a society like ours?

Bibliography

When *Children in Danger* was first published in May 1974 there were no British books on the battered baby syndrome. Until then the only books available were American:

HELFER, R., and KEMPE, H. (eds.) (1968), *The Battered Child*, University of Chicago Press.

KEMPE, H., and HELFER, R. (eds.) (1972), *Helping the Battered Child and his Family*, Blackwell and J. B. Lippincott & Co.

Since then the following have been published:

CARTER, J. (ed.) (1974), *The Maltreated Child*, Priory Press.

HOWELLS, J. G. (1974), *Remember Maria*, Butterworth.

Concerning Child Abuse: Papers Presented by the Tunbridge Wells Study Group on Non-Accidental Injury to Children (1975), Churchill Livingstone.

The following two publications by the NSPCC have been used extensively in my book:

CASTLE, R., and KERR, A. (1972), *A Study of Suspected Child Abuse*.

SKINNER, A., and CASTLE, R. (1969), *78 Battered Children: A Retrospective Study*.

There are many articles on the subject to be found in the various professional journals. I have quoted from the following:

CAMERON, J. M. (1972), 'The battered baby syndrome', *Practitioner*, Symposium on Forensic Medicine, September, vol. 209, pp. 302–10.

COURT, J. (1970), 'Psycho-social factors in child battering', *Journal of the Medical Women's Federation*, April, pp. 99–104.

COURT, J., and ROBINSON, W. (1970), 'The battered child

syndrome', *Midwives Chronicle and Nursing Notes*, July, pp. 212–16.

HALL, M. H. (1972), 'Non-accidental injuries in children', paper read before the Health Congress of the Royal Society of Health, Eastbourne, 24–28 April.

OKELL, C. (1969), 'The battered child – a tragic breakdown in parental care', *Midwife and Health Visitor*, June, pp. 235–40.

OKELL, C. (1971), 'Childhood accidents and child abuse', *Community Medicine*, 20 August, pp. 124–7.

OKELL, C., and BUTCHER, C. H. H. (1969), 'The battered child syndrome', *Law Society's Gazette*, September, pp. 587–9.

Two books which I found threw useful light on child abuse, one directly, one through its main theme, were:

BERRY, J. (1972), *Social Work with Children*, Routledge & Kegan Paul.

STORR, A. (1968), *Human Aggression*, Penguin Books.